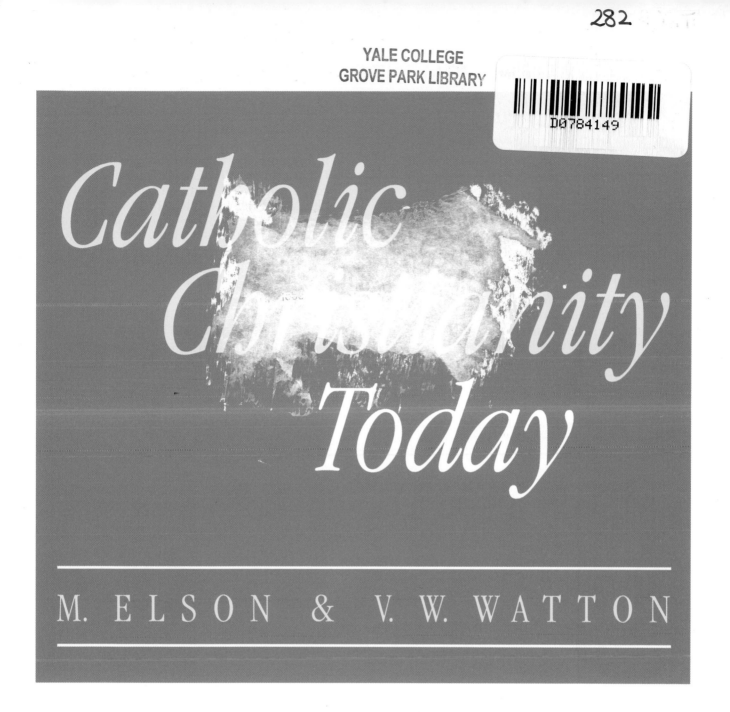

Catholic Christianity Today

M. ELSON & V. W. WATTON

Hodder & Stoughton

A MEMBER OF THE HODDER HEADLINE GROUP

ACKNOWLEDGEMENTS

Thanks to Jill for her photography and support. Thanks also to Maureen McGuigan; Vicky Hatton; Loran McCue; Shemik Ahmed and the Religious Studies students at Stockton Sixth Form College; St Michael's School, Billingham; Lyn Greenhow and the pupils of Langfield School.

The publishers would like to thank the following for permission to reproduce copyright material in this volume:

Cassell – Geoffrey Chapman (UK) and Veritas (Ireland) for extracts from *Catholic Catechism of the Catholic Church*; Darton, Longman & Todd for passages from *The New Jerusalem Bible, Study Edition* (1994); HarperCollins for extracts from *The Sunday Missal*; Oxford University Press for an extract from *The Spirtual Nature of Man* by Sir Alister Hardy.

The publishers would also like to thank the following for permission to reproduce copyright illustrations in this volume:

AKG London p22 (Santa Maria della Salute, Venice), 43 (Museo del Prado, Madrid), 64 (Prague National Gallery), 65 (Museo de Santa Cruz, Toledo), 71 (Palace of the Doge, Venice), 81 (Coll. Archiv f. Kunst & Geschichte, Berlin), 101 (Alte Pinakothek, Munich); Andes Press Agency/Carlos Reyes p12, 23, 28, 29, 31, 39, 41, 44, 48, 55, 67, 87, 102, 121, 123, 125; J. Catling Allen p16; Barnaby's Picture Library/H. Kanus p17; The Bridgeman Art Library p35; Buckfast Abbey p49; Corbis Bettmann/UPI p107; Tony Haynes p116;

Popperfoto p103, 111, 113 (Derek Ceyrac), 119, 128 (Roslan Rahman); Rex Features Ltd p92, 93 (Dennis Stone); The Library Committee of the Religious Society of Friends in Britain p52; The John Rylands University Library of Manchester p33, reproduced by courtesy of the Director and University Librarian; Science Photo Library p14 (Jean Lorre), 75; Shout Picture Agency p32, 40, 42, 45, 58, 60, 61, 62, 68, 83, 85, 97, 114, 118; Trip p66 (R Soar), 125 (A Barrett); Jill Watton p9, 10, 53, 55, 72, 94, 95, 97, 126; © Yorkshire Television Limited p16.

Every effort has been made to trace and acknowledge copyright. The publishers will be glad to make suitable arrangements with any copyright holders whom it has not been possible to contact.

For our wives Verity and Jill.

British Library Cataloguing in Publication Data

Watton, Victor W.
    Catholic Christianity today
    1.Catholic Church
    I.Title II.Elson, M.
    282

ISBN 0 340 664118

First published 1997
Impression number   10 9 8 7 6 5 4 3 2 1
Year   2000 1999 1998 1997

Printed in Great Britain for Hodder & Stoughton Educational, a division of Hodder Headline Plc 338 Euston Road, London NW1 3BH by Scotprint, Musselburgh, Scotland.

CONTENTS

PREFACE

This book is designed for Catholic students preparing for the GCSE Religious Studies courses and those preparing for the RE short courses in Catholic Christianity.

In conjunction with the *Teacher's Handbook*, it provides a complete resource for those preparing for the London Examinations and NEAB GCSE courses in Catholic Christianity.

Each chapter is divided into numbered factfiles and the matrix on page 7 demonstrates how each syllabus can be covered by using particular factfiles.

Some alternative viewpoints are given from within the Christian tradition, but there are no critical views. It is hoped that this will encourage students to think for themselves. The *Teacher's Handbook* explores these issues and gives guidance in the difficult area of evaluation.

As the London Examinations Syllabus Paper 1 is 'Religion and Life from a Catholic Perspective', parts of *Religion and Life* by Victor W. Watton have been incorporated in this text after editing to ensure the topic is presented from the Catholic perspective. Quotations from the *Catechism of the Catholic Church* are identified by the paragraph number in the eighth edition. Scriptures quoted are from *The New Jerusalem Bible*.

We hope that this textbook will help both schools and students to enjoy discovering the nature and relevance of Catholic Christianity to today's world.

EXAM BOARD MATRIX

LONDON EXAM BOARD

Paper 1	Believing in God	Factfiles 1, 2, 3, 4
	Matters of Life and Death	Factfiles 25, 26, 27, 28
	Marriage and Family Life	Factfiles 33, 34, 35, 36
	Social Harmony	Factfiles 37, 38, 39
Options	Religion and the Media	Factfiles 49, 50, 51, 52
	Catholicism: Wealth and Poverty	Factfiles 53, 54, 55, 56
Paper 2	Beliefs and Values	Factfiles 5, 6, 7, 8
	Traditions	Factfiles 9, 10, 11, 12
	Sacraments	Factfiles 13, 14, 15, 16
	Loving One's Neighbour	Factfiles 29, 31, 32
Options	Catholic Church at World Level	Factfiles 41, 42, 43, 44
	Christian Vocation	Factfiles 45, 46, 47, 48

NEAB

Paper 1	Public Worship	Factfiles 14, 15, 17, 18, 19, 20
	Pilgrimage	Factfile 24
	Private Worship	Factfiles 2, 6, 12, 46
	Festivals	Factfiles 21, 22, 23
	Apostle's Creed	Factfiles 5, 6, 7, 8, 9, 25
	The Bible	Factfile 11
Paper 2	Sacraments	Factfiles 13, 14, 15, 16, 25
	Attitudes to Death	Factfiles 25, 26
	Christian Values	Factfiles 29, 30
	Vocation	Factfiles 45, 46, 47, 48
	Justice and Peace	Factfiles 37, 38, 39, 40, 53, 54, 56
	Personal Issues	Factfiles 8, 16, 33, 34, 35, 26, 27, 28

INTRODUCTION

All the syllabuses require you to study Catholic Christianity in the context of Christianity as a whole. This introduction explains what the different Christian groups are, and why they are different.

Historical background

Christians believe that God created the world and made humans, in his image, to be his stewards of the world. They believe that God chose the Jewish people to be his special people who were to show the rest of the world (the Gentiles) how to live. When the Jews failed to do this properly, God sent his son, Jesus, to show people how to live and to save them from their sins.

Jesus and the early Christians were Jews, but most Jews did not become Christians, and so Christianity began to develop as a separate religion which was soon mainly Gentile.

Christians believe that Jesus is alive in the Christian Church which has developed since his death and resurrection and which is now the most numerous and widespread world religion.

Why there are differences of opinion among Christians

- Christianity developed in different places in different ways. By the time Christianity became the official religion of the Roman Empire in 356 CE, there were several different traditions within Christianity. They were organised mainly by bishops and councils of bishops, but in the West, the Bishop of Rome (the Pope) gradually became accepted as leader. In 1054 the Eastern Churches (Orthodox) ruled by councils of bishops split from the Western Church (Roman Catholic) which accepted the leadership of the Pope.

- In the sixteenth century, men like Martin Luther and John Calvin decided the Western Church had deviated from the Church of the New Testament. They protested and demanded reforms (the Reformation). This led to the Protestant or Reformed Churches, which believed in the Church being ruled democratically (all Christian believers being equal and being priests) and in the absolute authority of the Bible (individual Christians to interpret the Bible for themselves).

- The Church of England, established by Henry VIII and Elizabeth I, is a mixture of Protestant and Catholic ideas. English Protestants who would not join the Church of England are called Nonconformists.

- Another cause of difference since the nineteenth century has been liberal Christians who believe Christianity needs to take account of science and reason. They do not believe that the Bible should be taken literally as the word of God and reject many traditional beliefs.

The key features of non-Catholic Churches

The Orthodox Churches
These are national Churches led by a chief bishop called a Patriarach. Most of them are based in Eastern Europe (Greece, Russia, Rumania, Serbia). They have priests who may marry, but their bishops must be celibate. Their worship is very elaborate and they use icons and incense.

The Church of England
This is the state Church in England. The Queen is the head of the Church and appoints bishops. The Church of England has branches in all the English-speaking parts of the world. These Churches are independent but meet together at the Lambeth Conference which is always chaired by the Archbishop of Canterbury. These Churches are known as either Anglican or Episcopalian. Some are very Protestant and are called Low Church, others are very Catholic and are called High Church.

Nonconformist Churches
These are Churches which thought the Church of England was not Protestant enough. Instead of bishops or priests they have ministers who are regarded as no different from lay people. They are governed by democratically elected bodies and their services are Bible-based rather than communion-based. The main Nonconformist Churches are: the Methodist, the United Reformed (URC), the Baptist (who baptise adults rather than babies), the Society of Friends (Quakers), Pentecostals and a variety of Black Churches.

Examples:

Orthodox, Roman Catholic and some fundamentalists do not allow women priests, other Christians do.

Roman Catholics do not allow contraception, other Christians do.

Charismatics and many fundamentalists believe it is right to try to convert members of other religions, other Christians do not.

Some Christians believe homosexuality is condemned by God, others do not.

An early Methodist church built in 1762.

How Christians make moral decisions

- All Christians believe that moral decisions should be based on the teachings of Jesus in the New Testament and the Ten Commandments in the Old Testament.

- ROMAN CATHOLICS believe that these teachings are best interpreted by the Church, especially the Head of the Church, the Pope, and the bishops. So, to make moral decisions, they may refer to the teachings of the Church contained in the *Catechism of the Catholic Church* (1994) or Encyclicals (long letters containing the Pope's teachings).

- ORTHODOX CHRISTIANS would base their decisions on how the Bible has been interpreted by councils of bishops, or simply ask advice from their priest (many Catholics would also do this).

- PROTESTANTS (Church of England, Methodist, Baptist, Pentecostal etc.) believe that each individual should make their own decision on the basis of what the Bible says, but most would also be guided by decisions made by democratically elected bodies of Church leaders (e.g. the General Synod of the Church of England or the Conference of the Methodist Church).

Many Anglican churches like this one date from before the Reformation.

BELIEVING IN GOD

Introduction

This chapter is concerned with the reasons people have for believing, or not believing in God.

Some people may be led to believe in God for many reasons; others may believe for one reason and when they discover other reasons for believing in God, they find them helpful in supporting their belief in God.

There is no factfile on why people find it difficult to believe in God, you will have to discuss this, then receive a revision file from your teacher.

If you are brought up as a Catholic, you learn about God from a very early age. You would be baptised and, to keep the promises they made at your baptism, your parents would probably teach you prayers as soon as you could talk.

Next you would go to Children's Liturgies where you would learn more about God and how he made and looks after you. You would say prayers to God thanking him for looking after you and so it would seem natural to you to believe in God.

You would also be taken to church by your parents, especially at Christmas and Easter, and at church you would hear people talking about God and assuming that God exists.

All these teachings would be confirmed when you started school and there were assemblies, home-time prayers, and RE lessons in which teachers referred to the things you had heard at home and at church. Your first communion and later your confirmation would encourage you to believe in God.

FACTFILE 1

CATHOLIC UPBRINGING AND BELIEF IN GOD

"I am a Catholic because I was born to Catholic parents and I was educated in a Catholic school. All my upbringing made me believe in God and I have never really thought that God might not exist. God is a part of my life just as my parents and friends are."

A Catholic adult.

How can you tell this is a Catholic school?

RELIGIOUS EXPERIENCE AND BELIEF IN GOD

Most people who have a religious upbringing believe in God and find that their own religious experience supports and confirms that belief.

Religious experience can be defined in many ways, but the most common are:

- the feeling you get when you enter a great religious building or even a beautiful place, a feeling of awe and wonder, a feeling that there is something greater than you which you can only call God (a famous scholar, Rudolf Otto, called this 'the numinous');
- the feeling that there is something inside you wanting you to change your life and be more committed to your religion (some scholars call this 'conversion experience');
- a belief that a miracle has happened and that it must have been caused by God;
- a belief that your prayers have been answered (this is often connected to miracles, e.g. if a Catholic prays for her mother to be cured of cancer and she is, she will believe both that her prayers have been answered and that God has caused a miracle to happen – both of which will lead her to believe that God exists);
- an experience where you feel that you have been in contact with God in a special way (this is often called 'mystical' and can include having a very strong numinous experience, going into trances, or having visions).

Followers of all religions have experiences like these which lead them to believe that God exists.

"My daughter, Joan, was killed by a car when she was seven years old. She and I were very close and I was grief stricken. She was lying in her coffin in her bedroom, I fell on my knees by the bedside. Suddenly I felt as if something a bit behind me was so overcome with pity that it was consolidating itself. Then I felt a touch on my shoulder lasting only an instant, and I knew there was another world."

Incident from the files of the Religious Experience Research Unit published in 'The Spiritual Nature of Man', Sir Alister Hardy.

Father Yves Dubois has had clear experiences of the reality of God ... Not only the strong feelings of the presence of God which he often feels for example at services, but, "Exceptional experiences of knowing that Jesus was present in the room in a special way. Twice also I have experienced the certainty of the presence of the Mother of God, which was an awareness of purity, holiness and love unlike anything I have ever known. Her holiness would have been frightening but for the strong feeling of love and compassion."

Interview quoted in 'Christians in Britain Today'.

"All my experience of religion has convinced me that God exists. I know when I pray that God is listening to me. I feel at the Mass that Christ enters me."

A Catholic adult.

Miracles

Most religious people believe in miracles.

By 'a miracle', they usually mean 'an event which seems to break a natural law and for which the only explanation is God'.

Some religious people think that a miracle is 'a natural event which must be caused by God because of the time at which it occurs and the religious connections it has'.

In August 1879, an image of the Virgin Mary, along with St Joseph and St John the Evangelist, appeared on the outside wall of the Catholic church in the Irish village of Knock. It was seen by at least fifteen different villagers. They all stated that: it was very bright; it reached almost to the ground; when they tried to touch the figures, all they could feel was the wall. It could not have been a projection because when the villagers stood in front of the figures, they cast no shadows on the wall.

They could think of no explanation except that this was a miracle and it reinforced their belief in God because, if he can make a miracle happen, he must exist.

In the same way in the Gospels, when Jesus healed lepers, gave sight to the blind and raised the dead, people began to believe that God was acting through him, because there seemed to be no other explanation for what was happening.

Many religious believers think that miracles still happen today. Quite often at Christian healing services, people suffering from incurable cancers are healed. They, and the people who have prayed for them, believe they have been healed by God performing a miracle.

If miracles happen, then they are obviously a reason for believing in God, because God must exist if they happen!

The Shrine at Knock – a place of pilgrimage and healing.

FACTFILE 3

EXPERIENCE OF THE WORLD AND BELIEF IN GOD

If you came across a watch in an uninhabited place, you could not say it had been put there by chance. The complexity of its mechanism would make you say it had a designer. The universe is far more complex than a watch and so if a watch needs a watchmaker, the universe needs a universe maker and that could only be God.

Abridged from 'Natural Theology', William Paley.

Many people look at the world, the solar system, the universe and feel that it all appears to be designed. For example:
- the way DNA is so carefully structured that a tiny fertilised human egg (almost invisible to the naked eye) is the blueprint for an adult human being;
- the way in which the Big Bang (the cosmic explosion which many scientists believe was the beginning of the universe) was so designed – the size and timing of the explosion, the laws of gravity and the nature of matter – that human life was bound to evolve;
- all this implies that there is design in the universe and if there is design, there must be a designer, and who could that be but God?

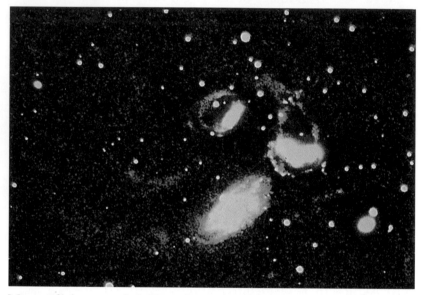

Many religious people believe that only God could have set off the Big Bang to start the Universe.

The question about the origins of the world and of man has been the object of many scientific studies which have splendidly enriched our knowledge of the age and dimensions of the cosmos, the development of life-forms and the appearance of man. These discoveries invite us to even greater admiration for the greatness of the Creator ...

Catechism of the Catholic Church (283).

Other people look at the world and see that everything seems to have a cause. If everything has a cause, then it is logical to assume that the universe has a cause and that could only be God.

Science is based on the idea that everything has an explanation, things do not 'just happen'. If everything in the universe has an explanation, then it is reasonable to believe that the universe itself has an explanation, and the only possible explanation of the universe is God.

Other people find that their whole experience of life makes them believe that life has a purpose. Birth, marriage, careers, the way we need to love and be loved make them feel that we can't be here by chance. There must be a reason for us being here – life must have a purpose. It is in looking for a purpose in life that many people turn to religion and are led to believe in God.

Some people think that religion itself is evidence for God's existence. People have always had religious beliefs – the Stone Age cave paintings all depict forms of religion. There are also many similarities in religion:

- the idea of God as creator
- the belief that it is possible to get in touch with God
- the moral rules of religions
- the miracles and visions which occur in all religions
- prayer.

It may be that, just as the laws of science were there waiting to be discovered by scientists, so God is there waiting to be discovered by religion.

> The human person: With his openness to truth and beauty, his sense of moral goodness, his freedom and the voice of his conscience, with his longings for the infinite and for happiness, man questions himself about God's existence. In all this he discerns signs of his spiritual soul. The soul, the 'seed of eternity we bear in ourselves, irreducible to the merely material,' can have its origin only in God.

Catechism of the Catholic Church (33).

Evil and suffering are linked together because evil is wrong, and it usually causes suffering, e.g. attacking someone with a beer bottle is an evil action and causes suffering.

Philosophers often divide evil into two kinds:

MORAL EVIL – SUFFERING WHICH IS CAUSED BY HUMAN BEINGS DOING WRONG THINGS AS IN THE BEER BOTTLE EXAMPLE.

NON-MORAL/NATURAL EVIL – SUFFERING WHICH IS CAUSED BY THE WAY THINGS ARE IN THE WORLD, E.G. THE SUFFERING CAUSED BY AN EARTHQUAKE.

> Evil and suffering cause problems for religious believers because:
>
> - If God is good, he must want to eliminate suffering.
>
> - If God is all-knowing, he must have known what suffering would result from creating the world.
>
> - If God is all-powerful, he must be able to prevent or eliminate suffering.
>
> As there is suffering in the world, it would appear that God cannot be good and all-knowing and all-powerful.
>
> As most religious believers believe that God is all-knowing, all-powerful and good, this is bound to cause them a problem.

FACTFILE 4

EVIL AND SUFFERING

How can God allow mothers to die when their babies need them?

Christian responses to evil and suffering

Christians respond to suffering in many different ways. Some are practical, others are more theoretical and many Christians would combine the two.

The main response of Christians to suffering is a practical one – to help those who are suffering.
This is done either by:
- PRAYER (asking God to help those who are suffering – such prayer is called intercession and is a feature of nearly every Christian act of worship)

or by
- SERVICE (actively helping those who suffer) – many Christians help in hospitals and hospices, organise food and clothing for down and outs in Great Britain, raise money to help less developed countries etc. This is often done in response to Jesus' teaching in the parable of the sheep and the goats.

> **Then the upright will say to him in reply, "Lord when did we see you hungry and feed you, or thirsty and give you drink? When did we see you a stranger and make you welcome, lacking clothes and clothe you? When did we see you sick or in prison and go to see you?" And the King will answer, "In truth I tell you, in so far as you did this to one of the least of these brothers of mine, you did it to me."**

The parable of the sheep and the goats, Matthew 25:37-40.

This shrine at Lourdes is visited by thousands of suffering Christians, some of whom believe that they are cured by God.

- Many Christians connect the idea of **free will** with evil and suffering. According to *Genesis* 1, God created us in his image which means he created us with free will. He wants us to be free people who decide for ourselves whether to believe in God or not. To be free means free to do either good or evil, and so God could not have created free people who always did the good. Evil and suffering are caused by human misuse of free will and so are not the fault of God.

- Other Christians point out that this world was not created as a paradise. God created this world as **a preparation for paradise**. Paradise comes in heaven after we die. So in this world we have to live in such a way that we improve our souls and become good enough to enter paradise. These Christians also believe that to do good requires evil – I cannot share my wealth if there are no poor people. So God made this world with the possibility of evil, but there will be no evil or suffering in the next world.

- Many Christians believe there is no point in worrying about the problem because **we cannot understand God's reasons** for doing things. God must have a reason for allowing evil and suffering, but we cannot know what it is because we are not God. However, we do know from the life of Jesus that even God's own Son had to suffer, and that Jesus commanded his followers to respond to suffering by helping those who suffer. Jesus healed the sick, fed the hungry and even raised the dead, and we should respond in the same way – by helping to remove suffering.

> Then I saw a new heaven and a new earth; the first heaven and the first earth had disappeared now, and there was no longer any sea. I saw the holy city, the new Jerusalem, coming down out of heaven from God, prepared as a bride dressed for her husband. Then I heard a loud voice call from the throne, "Look here, God lives among human beings. He will make his home among them, they will be his people, and he will be their God, God-with-them. He will wipe away all tears from their eyes; there will be no more death, and no more mourning or sadness or pain. The world of the past has gone."

Revelation 21:1-4.

> By the grace of this sacrament (of Anointing) the sick person receives the strength and the gift of uniting himself more closely to Christ's Passion: in a certain way he is *consecrated* to bear fruit by configuration to the Saviour's redemptive Passion. Suffering, a consequence of original sin, acquires a new meaning: it becomes a participation in the saving work of Jesus.

Catechism of the Catholic Church (1521).

Auschwitz concentration camp is a permanent reminder of the crimes carried out by the Nazis' misuse of their free will.

QUESTIONS

Factfile 1 Catholic Upbringing and Belief in God

1 Have a class discussion on what parts of a religious upbringing are likely to make you believe in God and whether any of it might turn you against God.

Factfile 2 Religious Experience

1 Write your definition of a religious experience.

2 Explain how a religious experience might make you believe in God.

3 How else could a religious experience be explained?

Factfile 3 Experience of the World

1 Divide a page into two columns headed 'Believe in God' and 'Not believe in God'. Then go through people's experiences of the world and put them into one of the columns. You will need to think about what goes into the second column, as this is not given in the book!

Factfile 4 Evil and Suffering

1 Write down in your own words why the existence of evil and suffering in the world makes it difficult to believe in God.

2 Write two Christian responses to the problem of evil and suffering.

3 Discuss in a group whether these responses succeed in dealing with the problem.

4 'Miracles don't happen nowadays.' Do you agree? Give reasons for your answer, showing that you have considered another point of view. You should use information from the whole chapter in answering this question.

BELIEFS AND VALUES

The main Christian beliefs are found in the Apostles' Creed which Christians recite as a list of their beliefs at various services. The creed is:

> I believe in God, the Father almighty, creator of heaven and earth.
>
> I believe in Jesus Christ, his only Son, our Lord. He was conceived by the power of the Holy Spirit and born of the Virgin Mary. He suffered under Pontius Pilate, was crucified, died, and was buried. He descended to the dead. On the third day he rose again. He ascended into heaven, and is seated at the right hand of the Father. He will come again to judge the living and the dead.
>
> I believe in the Holy Spirit, the holy catholic Church, the communion of saints, the forgiveness of sins, the resurrection of the body, and the life everlasting.

The creed begins with, 'I believe in God'. This means Christians believe in only one God who is unlimited (infinite) and eternal. This belief in one God is known as **monotheism**.

Christians refer to God as their father because Jesus taught that God is our father – God made us as his children and we can have a relationship with God similar to the relationship children have with their father. However, unlike an earthly father, God will never let us down and will always be there to give us the guidance and protection we would like from our earthly fathers. This is particularly shown in the Lord's Prayer where Jesus taught his followers to speak to God as our father. Because God is our father, he must love us and God shows his love in sending Jesus to save us from our sins, and in all the wonderful gifts of life on earth.

Christians also believe that God is almighty. God is all-powerful and can do whatever he wants. As Christians say at the end of the Lord's Prayer, 'For yours is the kingdom, the power and the glory'.

As our all-powerful father, God created the world in six days and created humans in his image. When Jesus spoke of God, he referred to God as understood in the tradition of the Jewish people. For Christians this means the God of the Old Testament which begins by stating that God is the creator (*Genesis* 1:1–2:3).

FACTFILE 5

GOD THE FATHER

(Jesus) said to them, "When you pray, this is what to say:
'Father, may your name be held holy,
your kingdom come;
give us each day our daily bread,
and forgive us our sins,
for we ourselves forgive each one who is in debt to us.
And do not put us to the test.' "

Luke 11:2-4.

Genesis 1:1–2:3 says that God created in this way:
Day 1 – light to separate night from day;
Day 2 – the sky to separate the waters;
Day 3 – dry land and seas, vegetation (plants and trees);
Day 4 – sun, moon and stars;
Day 5 – fish and birds;
Day 6 – animals, creeping things, humans;
Day 7 – God rested and declared the seventh day a holy day.
'God saw all that he had made, and it was very good.'

For Christians the world and human beings do not just exist, they have an explanation and a purpose. They believe that all that God created is good and that human beings are the summit of his creation. God made human beings in his own image which means that humans have freedom and responsibility. They are free to believe in God and do what he says, or reject him.

God did not just make earth, he also made heaven and this part of the creed reminds Christians that God intends life on earth to be a preparation for eternal life in heaven (for more detail see factfile 25).

The supreme being must be unique, without equal. If God is not one, he is not God. Faith in God leads us to turn to him alone as our first origin and our ultimate goal, and neither to prefer anything to him nor to substitute anything for him.

Catechism of the Catholic Church (228-229).

FACTFILE 6

JESUS

At the time appointed by God, the only Son of the Father, the eternal Word, that is, the Word and substantial Image of the Father, became incarnate; without losing his divine nature, he has assumed human nature.

Catechism of the Catholic Church (479).

Mary is truly 'Mother of God' since she is mother of the eternal Son of God made man, who is God himself.

Catechism of the Catholic Church (509).

Christians believe that Jesus:
is the only son of God
Jesus is not separate from God. When Jesus was born, God appeared in human form to show people his nature and to die for their sins. Jesus becoming human is called the **Incarnation** – God coming in flesh. Christians believe that Jesus has two natures, human and divine in one person. This is the great mystery of Jesus' life.

was born of the Virgin Mary
Christians refer to Mary as 'the Mother of God' because, through Mary, God became human in Jesus. They believe that she remained a virgin and that through her immaculate conception she was free from original sin.

suffered under Pontius Pilate, was crucified, died and was buried
Jesus lived at a particular time in history and so his death is remembered by the name of the historical Roman governor of Judea, Pontius Pilate. It was a real death because he was crucified, he died, and he was buried. Christians believe that the death of Jesus was part of God's plan. Jesus is called the Christ (the Greek form of the Hebrew, Messiah) because he was God's Anointed One, the one chosen to take away the sins of the world through his death on the cross.

descended to the dead
This is another reminder that it was a real death which included the suffering needed to forgive our sins.

on the third day he rose again

Because Jesus was God, death was not the end. Christians believe that having suffered for our sins and died, Jesus rose from the dead. They believe that the risen Jesus was with them and could even pass through walls and locked doors. Christians also believe that his resurrection is a promise that they too will rise from the dead.

ascended into heaven and is seated at the right hand of the Father

Christ's risen body was taken to heaven where he is with the Father, constantly interceding for humans. The Church is seen as the body of Christ on earth, although its head, Jesus, is now in heaven.

will come again to judge the living and the dead

Christians believe that at the end of time Jesus will return for the final judgement when all people will be brought before Jesus and he will judge them on the basis of the deeds and faith the secrets of which only he knows.

> Jesus Christ, the Head of the Church, precedes us into the Father's glorious kingdom so that we, the members of his Body, may live in the hope of one day being with him forever.

Catechism of the Catholic Church (666).

> Jesus freely offered himself for our salvation. Beforehand, during the Last Supper, he both symbolized this offering and made it really present: 'This is my body which is given for you'.

Catechism of the Catholic Church (621).

> Christ the first born from the dead is the principle of our own resurrection.

Catechism of the Catholic Church (658).

FACTFILE 7

THE HOLY SPIRIT

'Effusion of the Holy Spirit' by Titian.

The Apostles' Creed next states that Christians believe in the **Holy Spirit**. Spirit is a translation of the Hebrew 'ruah' meaning 'air', 'breath', 'life', and the Holy Spirit is God's presence in the world. Catholics believe the Holy Spirit is present in everything the Church does and is what 'inspires' Christians. The Holy Spirit is also how God gives life to and rules his creation. So the Holy Spirit can be thought of as God's activity in the world.

> The Holy Spirit, whom Christ the Head pours out on his members, builds, animates and sanctifies the Church.

Catechism of the Catholic Church (747).

The Church has many **symbols for the Holy Spirit**:
•fire •cloud • the dove • and, in baptism, water.
Christians believe that Jesus' greatest gift to his followers was his gift of the Spirit through which God can come into our hearts. This is seen particularly in the sacraments – the mighty works of God which bear fruit in the new life in Christ.

Christians, like Jews and Muslims, believe in only one God, but they believe that God reveals himself in three ways – as Father, as Son and as Holy Spirit. This is known as **the Trinity**.

This means that God is three in one and one in three. The Church teaches that there are three persons in God (Father, Son and Holy Spirit) and yet only one substance – God. This is the great mystery of the Christian faith which is beyond human understanding and yet Christians know from their experience of God that he is three persons and yet is only one God.

> The Trinity is One. We do not confess three Gods, but one God in three persons, the consubstantial Trinity. The divine persons do not share the one divinity among themselves but each of them is God, whole and entire: 'The Father is that which the Son is, the Son that which the Father is, the Father and the Son that which the Holy Spirit is, i.e. by nature one God'.

Catechism of the Catholic Church (253).

> The Church ... is the place where we know the Holy Spirit:
>
> – in the Scriptures he inspired;
> – in the Tradition to which the Church Fathers are always timely witnesses;
> – in the Church's *Magisterium* which he assists;
> – in the sacramental liturgy, through its words and symbols, in which the Holy Spirit puts us into communion with Christ;
> – in prayer, wherein he intercedes for us;
> – in the charisms and ministries by which the Church is built up;
> – in the signs of apostolic and missionary life;
> – in the witness of saints.

Catechism of the Catholic Church (688).

The Apostles' Creed ends with the words:
I believe in
- the holy catholic Church, the communion of saints (see factfile 9)
- the forgivness of sins (see factfile 16)
- the resurrection of the body and the life everlasting (see factfile 25).

The need for repentance and faith

The Gospels state that the public ministry of Jesus began when he met John the Baptist. Christians believe that John was the forerunner of Jesus, that he prepared the way for him. John called on people to repent. **Repentance** means completely changing one's life for the better. John told the people who came to him to give up their evil ways and, as a sign of this, he baptised them in the River Jordan.

When the first Christians began to proclaim their beliefs, they told their listeners to 'repent and believe the gospel'. By the word 'gospel' they meant the good news of what God had done for human beings through the life and death of Jesus. Belief in the gospel is what Christians mean by faith. A person becomes a Christian through faith: this means accepting the truth of the claims made about Jesus as to who he is (the Son of God) and what he did (the Saviour who saved the world from sin). Christians show their faith in Jesus by joining the community of believers, the Church.

Forgiveness of sins and reconciliation

Christians believe that all human beings (except Jesus) have been and are sinful. Everyone does wrong and because wrongdoing is offensive to God, everyone needs forgiveness. Christians believe that the killing of Jesus represented human wrongdoing at its worst. They see his death as a unique moment in human history. It provided the opportunity and motive for people to be saved from their sins. Christians believe that the death of Jesus was part of God's plan and the means by which the forgiveness of sins is achieved.

Sin separates human beings from God. Christians believe that the death of Jesus has saved people from the power of sin and their faith in this reconciles them to God. In other words, Jesus' death looks like the triumph of evil over good, but it is the exact opposite: the goodness of Jesus was not destroyed by his death, but lives on in his followers. So the death of Jesus removed the distance from God caused by sin and this is what Christians mean by **reconciliation**. For Catholics, this reconciliation is achieved primarily through baptism and renewed through the sacrament of penance and celebration of the Mass.

Reconciliation is shown in the story of Zachaeus, a cheat, who showed his faith in Jesus by climbing a tree to see him. Jesus invited himself to Zachaeus' house for a meal and Jesus' love for Zachaeus showed him his sins and he repaid everyone he had cheated. So by faith Zachaeus' sins were forgiven by Jesus, and Zachaeus was reconciled with God and with the people he had wronged.
(Luke 19:1-9.)

FACTFILE 8

SIN AND SALVATION

Sin is above before all else an offence against God, a rupture of communion with him.

Catechism of the Catholic Church (1440).

Christians believe that Jesus' death brought about reconciliation.

The confession (or disclosure) of sins, even from a simply human point of view, frees us and facilitates our reconciliation with others. Through such an admission, man looks squarely at the sins he is guilty of, takes responsibility for them, and thereby opens himself again to God and to the communion of the Church.

Catechism of the Catholic Church (1455).

> Faith is first of all a personal adherence of man to God. At the same time, and inseparably, it is a free assent to the whole truth that God has revealed. As personal adherence to God and assent to his truth, Christian faith differs from our faith in any human person.
>
> *Catechism of the Catholic Church (150).*

Love of God and love of others

Jesus was once asked the question, 'What is the greatest commandment?'. This is a very difficult question to answer and most Catholics would probably answer with the words of Jesus which are based on *Deuteronomy* 6:5.

> "This is the first: 'Listen, Israel, the Lord our God, is the one, only Lord, and you must love the Lord your God with all your heart, with all your soul, with all your mind and with all your strength.' The second is this: 'You must love your neighbour as yourself.' There is no other commandment greater than these."

(Mark 12:29-31).

So the supreme Christian value is love, love of God and love of others. People achieve their destiny as human beings by loving God above everything. This means that human values should take second place for Christians. It is God's values which show Christians how to live their lives and they do this by loving God (by worshipping him and by being a member of his Church), and by loving others.

> One cannot honour another person without blessing God his creator. One cannot adore God without loving all men, his creatures.
>
> *Catechism of the Catholic Church (2069).*

Christians are to love others as Jesus explained when a scribe asked him what he had to do to inherit eternal life. Jesus asked the scribe what the Jewish law said. The scribe used the same words from *Deuteronomy* Jesus used to answer the question about the greatest commandment, and Jesus said that he had answered correctly. However, the scribe asked Jesus to explain what it meant to love your neighbour. Jesus explained with the **parable of the Good Samaritan**. In this parable Jesus showed that your neighbour is anyone who is in trouble or needs your help regardless of their race or religion (see *Luke* 10:25-37).

In another **parable, the sheep and the goats,** Jesus explained that Christians will be judged on the Last Day on the basis of how they have helped those in need. There are examples in the parable: giving food to the hungry, drink to the thirsty and clothes to the naked, welcoming the stranger and visiting a person who is sick or in prison. Those who have done such things are surprised to be told, 'As you did it to one of the least of my brothers, you did it to me.' These people are blessed and receive their reward in heaven. Those who did not know that by refusing to help people in need they were refusing to help Jesus are shocked; they are cursed and receive their punishment in hell. The punishment is not for doing wrong, but for failing to show love for God by loving other people.

> Jesus shares the life of the poor, from the cradle to the cross; he experiences hunger, thirst and privation. Jesus identifies with the poor of every kind and makes active love towards them the condition of entering his kingdom.

Catechism of the Catholic Church (544).

Questions

Factfile 5 God the Father

1 What does the Apostles' Creed say about the nature of God?

2 What do Christians believe about God's creation?

Factfile 6 Jesus

1 What does the Apostles' Creed say about Jesus?

2 "Jesus was just a special man." Do you agree? Give reasons for your answer, showing you have considered another point of view.

Factfile 7 The Holy Spirit

1 What do Christians believe is the role of the Holy Spirit?

2 Name three symbols for the Holy Spirit.

3 What do Christians mean by the Trinity?

Factfile 8 Sin and Salvation

1 What other beliefs are there in the Apostles' Creed ?

2 "You don't need to be a Christian to lead a good life." Do you agree? Give reasons for your answer showing you have considered another point of view.

③ TRADITIONS

THE CHURCH

> The Church in her doctrine, life, and worship perpetuates and transmits to every generation that all she herself is, all that she believes.

Catechism of the Catholic Church (98).

> Salvation comes from God alone, but because we receive the life of faith through the Church, she is our mother. We believe the Church as the mother of our new birth, and not in the Church as if she were the author of our salvation.

Catechism of the Catholic Church (169).

Introduction

It is clear from the Gospels that Jesus intended that what he had begun should continue after his death. He chose disciples to be his followers and to learn from him. He appointed twelve of his followers to be apostles, that is, people sent by Jesus to go out and proclaim his message. Jesus started a new movement in which people were united by their shared faith in him. The movement Jesus started is what Christians mean by the Church. But Christians disagree about its organisation. Over the two thousand years since the time of Jesus there have been many disagreements in the Church. At first when Christians referred to different churches they meant the same church in different places. But now they may also mean different organisations of Christians in the same place.

The source of faith

Christianity has been handed down from the time of Jesus through the centuries to the present day. What has been handed down is faith in the Gospel of Jesus. A person who becomes a Christian joins the Church. Such a person receives and accepts the faith of the Church. Because the Church preserves the tradition from Jesus in its scriptures and through its worship, and by the proclamation of the Gospel, the Church is the source of faith for Christians. But Christians also say that faith is a gift that comes directly from God. One way of expressing this would be to say that faith comes from God through the church.

Means of salvation

Christians believe that human beings are sinful and that on their own they cannot stop being sinners. Experience of life suggests that people want to be good, but in practice they cannot achieve what they desire. Every day people do terrible things to each other. Christians claim that Jesus, through his life and death, showed that evil need not triumph but can be overcome. They believe that they have a way by which people can be saved from sin and become good. A person can achieve this through their faith which joins them to the whole Christian community. This is why Catholics speak of the Church as the means of salvation.

The Church is one

The people who believe in Jesus are united by this belief. All Christians share the same faith that Jesus is the son of God and their saviour. But in practice there are three main divisions in the Church. The first great division was between Catholic and Orthodox Christians. The second was the division between Catholic and Protestant Christians. Protestant Christians are further divided into different denominations such as Baptists and Methodists. Divisions in Christianity arose from different emphases of belief and have led to different forms of worship. Many Christians regret these divisions but also respect the richness and diversity of Christian life. This is the position of the ecumenical movement in Christianity. It is possible to treasure the variety but also seek to achieve greater Christian unity.

> The Church is one: she acknowledges one Lord, confesses one faith, is born of one Baptism, forms only one Body, is given life by the one Spirit, for the sake of one hope, at whose fulfilment all divisions will be overcome.

Catechism of the Catholic Church (866).

The Church is holy

Christians say that God is holy and that they want to become holy. To be holy is to be perfect as God is perfect and the way to achieve this, according to Jesus, is through his love. People must love God totally and love other human beings as much as they love themselves. Christians believe that they can become holy through faith in Jesus, by hope in a better future and through love of others. The Church regards itself as a community of people who are in the process of becoming holy. Christians see themselves as inheritors of the tradition of the Old Testament in which the Israelites believed themselves to be called by God to be a holy people. Christians believe that Jesus enabled Gentiles to follow his way so that the Church became a new and universal holy people. Christians also believe that God is at work in and through the Church and refer to this aspect of God as the Holy Spirit.

> The Church is holy: the Most Holy God is her author; Christ, her bridegroom, gave himself up to make her holy; the Spirit of holiness gives her life ... Her holiness shines in the saints ...

Catechism of the Catholic Church (867).

The Church is catholic

The Israelites believed that God was both their God and the God of the whole world and of all its people. They hoped that one day everybody, Jews and Gentiles, would accept this belief. Through Jesus and the early Christians this began to happen. They thought that everybody could believe in Jesus and become members of the Church. The Christian community was open to everybody and therefore, unlike the Jewish religion, it became universal. '**Catholic**' comes from from a Greek word which means exactly that, universal, and in that sense all Christians believe that the Church is catholic. It is important to recognise the difference between the catholic church and the Catholic Church. The Catholic Church is the largest group of Christians in the Church, but there are other major Churches such as the Orthodox Churches and the Protestant Churches. The distinguishing feature of the Catholic Church is that its members accept the leadership of the Pope, the bishop of Rome, as the successor of Saint Peter, the leader of the Apostles.

> The Church is catholic: she proclaims the fulness of the faith. She bears in herself and administers the totality of the means of salvation. She speaks to all men.

Catechism of the Catholic Church (868).

The Church is apostolic

> The Church is apostolic. She is built on a lasting foundation, 'the twelve apostles of the Lamb' (*Revelation* 21:14) ... She is upheld infallibly in the truth: Christ governs her through Peter and the other apostles, who are present in their successors, the Pope and the college of bishops.

Catechism of the Catholic Church (869).

Jesus had disciples who followed him. Disciple means learner and these disciples learned from Jesus. From his disciples Jesus chose apostles. The tradition is that he chose twelve apostles and that this corresponds with the twelve tribes of Israel. Apostle comes from a Greek word meaning a person sent out on a mission. The apostles were disciples of Jesus chosen by him to proclaim his message to the whole world. They went out to persuade people to become Christians and to join the Church. Without them the Church would not exist. In the Catholic Church bishops are regarded as the successors of the apostles because they too have to maintain and proclaim the message of Jesus. The Pope, the bishop of Rome, has special authority for Catholics because they believe that the leader of the apostles, St Peter, was the original bishop in Rome. His authority has been passed down through apostolic succession to the present Pope. Orthodox and Protestant Christians do not accept that the bishop of Rome has this special authority. Despite this, many still regard the Pope as an important person in the Christian tradition. But all Christians agree that the Church came into existence through the preaching of the first apostles of Jesus. The Church is apostolic because it proclaims the same message about Jesus as was proclaimed by the original apostles. Christians today still hope to convince people of the truth of the Gospel and to persuade people to become followers of Jesus. The Church has a message and a mission.

St Peter's Square in Rome.

The Church is the body of Christ

When Christians speak of the body of Christ they mean first of all the human body in which Jesus lived just as we live in our bodies. They remember particularly the way in which he died as his body was broken on the cross. They also refer to the bread received at holy communion as his body and to the wine as his blood. Christians believe that Jesus gave his life in accordance with God's plan and that although he really died, his death marks the beginning of new life. He was raised and this is known and felt by Christians through their new and shared life together. So Jesus lives on through his followers, lives still in the Church, which is his body on earth. The writing of St Paul in the New Testament is. the principal source of these ideas. Paul says that people become Christians, members of the Church, by being baptised into the body of Christ. He also says that by sharing the bread at holy communion Christians share in the body of Christ. Christians believe that they continue the work of Jesus and that the Church is the body of Christ on earth.

The Church is the communion of saints

Communion means shared life or united fellowship. Christians are individuals but together they have a sense of belonging which arises from shared belief and hope, and which is expressed through love. 'Saints' here does not refer to people who are given that title because they lived outstandingly holy lives. Every Christian is given the opportunity to become holy, every Christian has a calling from God to live a life of love based on faith. Christians also believe that their shared life is not just a human arrangement but a gift from God, so it does not end with death. Just as Jesus died but lives on, so will Christians continue to live after they have died. The Catholic Church emphasises this by asserting that some Christians lived such holy and loving lives on earth that they can be relied on and prayed to. This expresses the other meaning of saints. These are people who are an example to other Christians. The Catholic Church has a process called canonisation which identifies such people.

> Three aspects of the Church as the Body of Christ are to be more specifically noted: the unity of all her members with each other as a result of their union with Christ; Christ as head of the Body; and the Church as bride of Christ.

Catechism of the Catholic Church (789).

CHRISTIAN MINISTRY

Ministry comes from the Latin word for service. Christian ministry is the continuation of the work of Jesus in the Church and to the world. In the New Testament there is evidence of Christian men and women fulfilling many different types of ministry. As time went by, in an attempt to impose control, the Church found ways of authorising individuals to exercise different kinds of ministry. A distinction was made between the ordinary ministry of all Christians and the ordained ministry. Only men were admitted to the ordained ministry and there were three levels, or orders: bishops, priests and deacons. The Catholic Church speaks of these as holy orders and regards them as one of the seven sacraments.

> The very differences which the Lord has willed to put between the members of his body serve its unity and mission. For 'in the Church there is diversity of ministry, but unity of mission. To the apostles and their successors Christ has entrusted the office of teaching, sanctifying and governing in his name and by his power. But the laity are made to share in the priestly, prophetical, and kingly office of Christ; they have therefore, in the Church and in the world, their own assignment in the mission of the whole People of God.'

Catechism of the Catholic Church (873).

> The bishops, established by the Holy Spirit, succeed the apostles ... Helped by the priests, their co-workers, and by the deacons, the bishops have the duty of authentically teaching the faith, celebrating divine worship, above all the Eucharist, and guiding their Churches as true pastors.

Catechism of the Catholic Church (938-9).

Bishops

Bishop comes from a Greek word meaning overseer. A bishop has full responsibility for the Church in a particular area. To help him in this he appoints priests and deacons. Bishops are regarded as the successors of the apostles who were sent out by Jesus to continue his work. The specific area for which a bishop is responsible is a **diocese** and the place of the bishop is the **see.** The church of the bishop is a **cathedral** which is the main church of the diocese. Bishops have special authority because of their high level of responsibility. When difficulties arose among Christians, the bishops as the leaders met together in councils to make decisions that were regarded as binding. Bishops have individual responsibility for a diocese and collective responsibility for the Church as a whole.

Priests

Priest comes from a Greek word meaning elder. In the New Testament a church would have a number of older men who were respected. Bishops came to use such men to advise and assist them. Nowadays a priest would normally belong to a local church and would lead the church in worship. He would be ordained by his bishop who would give him power to administer the sacraments. Priests are ministers of all the sacraments except holy orders, which is always, and confirmation which is usually, limited to bishops. The area for which a priest is reponsible is called a **parish.** The parish priest may be assisted by another priest often called a **curate.**

Cardinal Hume concelebrates Mass with bishops and priests at Westminster Cathedral.

Deacons

Deacon comes from a Greek word meaning servant. The role of deacons in the Church is less clear than that of bishops and priests. Many Protestant Churches have deacons who assist the minister. Until the Church of England decided to ordain women as priests, women could only be ordained as deacons. In the Catholic Church the state of being a deacon, the diaconate, was until recently limited to men who were on the way to becoming priests. Vatican II restored the permanent diaconate. There are permanent deacons in the Catholic Church ordained to the ministry but not paid as full time ministers. Permanent deacons may be married but cannot preside at the Eucharist or give the sacrament of reconciliation.

The role of the laity

Laity comes from a Greek word meaning people. At first it meant all Christians as the people chosen by God. Later it came to mean all the people of the Church who were not chosen to be bishops, priests or deacons. Ordained ministers were held in high regard, as were monks and nuns, but ordinary Christians, who had to work for their living and were married with children, were regarded as spiritually inferior. Vatican II gave a change of emphasis. Catholics are encouraged to be more involved in the life of the Church through parish and pastoral councils. They are encouraged to see the spiritual dimension in their lives and to recognise their vocation in the secular world. The aim is that the laity should begin to see itself as in partnership with, rather than subordinate to the ordained ministry. Catholics have the right and duty to participate actively at Mass by consciously taking part in the rites, prayers and songs, and also by serving as readers, servers, members of the choirs, etc.

> Lay people share in Christ's priesthood: evermore united with him, they exhibit the grace of Baptism and Confirmation in all dimensions of their personal, family, social and ecclesial lives, and so fulfil the call to holiness addressed to all the baptized.

Catechism of the Catholic Church (941).

The celibacy of the clergy

To be celibate is to live without engaging in any sexual activity, to have no wife or husband and to have no children. The first Christian ministers were not required to be celibate. According to the Gospels, Jesus healed Peter's mother-in-law, so he must have been married. Paul was not married and asserted that it is better for some Christians not to marry. Over the centuries the Church saw that there were advantages if those who were leaders did not have the responsibilities of family life. Eventually, the Catholic Church required all its bishops and priests to be celibate. In the eastern Churches a married man may be ordained priest but a priest may not marry after ordination, nor may bishops be married. In the Church of England there are no such restrictions. Celibacy is not required of deacons as a condition of ordination in any Church. The celibacy of the clergy is not an essential requirement of the Christian religion but is a rule imposed by the Catholic Church and could be changed. There is a small number of married men, mainly former clergy from other Churches, who have become Catholics and then priests, working in the Catholic Church.

The ordination of women

For Catholics, ordination means the act by which one person confers on another the sacrament of holy orders. Ordination is initiation into the sacramental ministry. The official teaching of the Catholic Church is clear and emphatic that only a baptised male can validly receive ordination. Its teaching is reaffirmed in 'Ordinatio Sacerdotalis' (1994). The main argument is that Jesus chose only men to be his apostles and when they chose bishops and priests to continue their ministry they followed the choice of Jesus. The Catholic Church regards itself as bound by this choice, and so the ordination of women is not possible. Some scholars argue that there is evidence in the New Testament and in the tradition of the Church to support the idea that women may be deacons. There is an example in the New Testament of a woman deacon. Paul speaks of Phoebe 'our sister, a deacon of the Church at Cenchreae' (Romans 16:1). Some Catholics argue that if Paul, who was not always favourable to women, recognised a woman as a deacon then a woman could be a deacon today. Other Catholic scholars disagree. The leadership of the Catholic Church is also unlikely to agree to this. One major reason is that if a woman could validly receive the sacrament of holy orders by being ordained a deacon it would be difficult to see why she could not validly be ordained a priest or bishop. The question of the ordination of women has been controversial and divisive, and some Catholics want to continue discussing its possibility. The Catholic and Church of England positions are different and sadly prevent these two churches from being able to be fully united.

This wedding ceremony has been conducted by a woman. She is a minister of a non-Catholic church.

> The college of bishops, with whom the priests are united in the priesthood, makes the college of the twelve an ever-present and ever-active reality until Christ's return. The Church recognizes herself to be bound by this choice made by the Lord himself. For this reason the ordination of women is not possible.

Catechism of the Catholic Church (1577).

The Catholic Church believes it has the authority from God to teach the truth. Its authority and truth are based on three things: **the Bible**, **Tradition** and the **Magisterium**.

The Bible

The Church believes that the Bible is the direct revelation of God. God has spoken to us in the scriptures in words which we can understand, in the same way that God became human in Jesus so that he could live in a way we could understand.

The Church regards the Bible as holy, as the words of God. The Church refers to the books of the Bible as the Canon of Scripture. These books were written by men under the direct inspiration of the Holy Spirit so that they wrote exactly what God wanted written, no more and no less.

The Bible is tremendously important for Christians because:
* it is a record of God's actions in history from the creation of the universe in *Genesis*, through the history of the Jewish people and their prophecies about the Messiah, to the birth, life and death of Jesus, his resurrection and ascension and the birth of his Church;
* it contains God's commands on how we should behave in such things as the Ten Commandments and the Sermon on the Mount;
* it shows Christians all about God's only Son, Jesus, and all he did on earth.

The Bible is divided into:
* the **Old Testament** (which contains God's laws for the Jews, prophecies about the coming of Jesus, and the history of the Jewish people before Jesus) and
* the **New Testament** (which contains the four Gospels about the life and death of Jesus, the Acts of the Apostles about the founding of the Church, and letters of early Church leaders such as St Paul and St Peter).

Tradition

The Church believes that Christ commanded his apostles to preach the Gospel (Good News) that Jesus had risen from the dead and fulfilled the promises made by God through the prophets. The Gospel was handed on in two ways:
* **in writing** – by those who wrote God's message of salvation in the books of the Bible under the inspiration of the Holy Spirit;
* **orally** – by the Apostles in their preaching, examples and the institutions they established, e.g. the Apostles' Creed.

This oral Gospel has been passed on by the Apostles to the bishops and so on through the apostolic succession. So the Church in its doctrine, life and worship is able to keep the Apostolic Tradition as a living source of salvation.

Both Tradition and Scripture (the Bible) come from God and represent twin sources of authority for Christians.
It is the duty of the Church to interpret these two sources of authority to present day Christians through the *Magisterium*.

AUTHORITY AND TRADITION

> God is the author of Sacred Scripture because he inspired its human authors; he acts in them and by means of them. He thus gives assurance that their writings teach without error his saving truth.

Catechism of the Catholic Church (136).

The earliest fragment of John's Gospel, written in Greek on a piece of papyrus. It is in the John Rylands Library in Manchester.

> What Christ entrusted to the apostles, they in turn handed on by their preaching and writing, under the inspiration of the Holy Spirit, to all generations ...

Catechism of the Catholic Church (96).

The Magisterium

It is the duty of the Church to interpret these twin authorities for the life of Christian people today. This task of interpreting the beliefs and practices of the Church is carried out by the Pope and the college of bishops under his leadership.

This teaching office is called the **Magisterium** ('the living teaching office of the Church'). The Pope and the bishops are the ones who can define the beliefs of the Church (**dogmas**), the precepts of the Church and the moral beliefs of the Church which all Catholics should follow. Therefore, the *Magisterium* is the supreme authority for Catholics telling them what to believe and how to behave.

The Pope is responsible for the *Magisterium* and so is the ultimate authority for Catholics, but, since Vatican II, it has been accepted that the Pope should confer with the bishops who are successors of the apostles just as the Pope is the successor of St Peter.

Vatican II declared that no one should be forced to act against their conscience and this has been restated in the *Catechism* (*1782*). Some Catholics have claimed from this that if their conscience conflicts with the *Magisterium*, they should be allowed to follow their conscience. However, the *Catechism* makes clear that an individual's conscience can make mistakes, whereas the *Magisterium* cannot. Therefore, a Catholic believes that they should follow the teachings of the Church on faith (what we are to believe) and morals (what is right and what is wrong).

> The task of interpreting the Word of God authentically has been entrusted solely to the Magisterium of the Church, that is, to the Pope and to the bishops in communion with him.

Catechism of the Catholic Church (100).

> The Lord made St Peter the visible foundation of his Church. He entrusted the keys of the Church to him. The bishop of the Church of Rome, successor to St Peter, is 'head of the college of bishops, the Vicar of Christ and Pastor of the universal Church on earth.'

Catechism of the Catholic Church (936).

> The Roman Pontiff and the bishops, as authentic teachers, preach to the People of God the faith which is to be believed and applied in moral life. It is also incumbent on them to pronounce on moral questions that fall within the natural law and reason.
>
> The infallibility of the *Magisterium* of the Pastors extends to all the elements of doctrine, including moral doctrine, without which the saving truths of the faith cannot be preserved, expounded or observed.

Catechism of the Catholic Church (2050-51).

Catholics regard the Virgin Mary as a model of the Christian life and an essential part of Christian worship.

Mary is regarded as a model of the Christian life because:
- she freely agreed to bear God's Son;
- she gave herself entirely to serve her son so that redemption could come through him;
- she stood at the cross and shared in the intensity of Christ's suffering;
- she helped the beginning of the Church through her prayers and her association with the apostles.

Mary is regarded as worthy of particular devotion because:
- her conception was immaculate (i.e. she had no original sin);
- she was specially chosen by God to be the mother of Jesus;
- through the virgin birth, she gave birth to God and so she is 'the Mother of God';
- as the mother of Christ, she is also Mother of the Church as it is Christ's body;
- at the end of her life she was taken up to heaven (Assumption of the Blessed Virgin Mary);
- in heaven she is able to pray for the souls of Christians on earth;
- prayers can be offered to Mary because she said in the Magnificat (*Luke* 1:48), 'all generations will call me blessed';
- the feasts of the Church dedicated to Mary show she deserves devotion;
- devotion to Mary does not interfere with belief in Christ as Saviour because Mary only helps people, she is not a saviour.

> By her complete adherence to the Father's will, to his Son's redemptive work, and to every prompting of the Holy Spirit, the Virgin Mary is the Church's model of faith and charity.

Catechism of the Catholic Church (967).

The Church teaches devotion to the Virgin Mary through prayers and the Hail Mary, and recommends that Catholics should use her life as a model for their own.

> The Church's devotion to the Blessed Virgin is intrinsic to Christian worship. The Church rightly honours 'the Blessed Virgin with special devotion. From the most ancient times the Blessed Virgin has been honoured with the title of "Mother of God", to whose protection the faithful fly in all their dangers and needs ... This very special devotion ... differs essentially from the adoration which is given to the incarnate Word and equally to the Father and the Holy Spirit, and greatly fosters this adoration.' The liturgical feasts dedicated to the Mother of God and Marian prayer, such as the rosary, an 'epitome of the whole Gospel', express this devotion to the Virgin Mary.

Catechism of the Catholic Church (971).

THE VIRGIN MARY

A fifteenth-century image of the Virgin Mary holding the child Jesus, from a church in Venice.

> Finally the Immaculate Virgin, preserved free from all stain of original sin, when the course of her earthly life was finished, was taken up body and soul into heavenly glory, and exalted by the Lord as Queen over all things, so that she might be more fully conformed to her Son, the Lord of lords and conqueror of sin and death.

Catechism of the Catholic Church (966).

QUESTIONS

Factfile 9 The Church

1 Why do Catholics regard the Church as the means of salvation?

2 Explain what Catholics mean when they say the Church is
a) catholic, b) apostolic, c) the Body of Christ.

3 "You don't have to go to church to be a Christian." Do you agree? Give reasons for your answer, showing you have considered another point of view.

Factfile 10 Christian Ministry

1 Explain the difference between bishop, priest and deacon.

2 What is the celibacy of the clergy and why do Catholics believe in it?

3 What is the role of the laity in the Catholic Church?

Factfile 11 Authority and Tradition

1 What is the apostolic succession?

2 What are the two sources of authority for Catholics and who has the authority to interpret them?

3 Explain why Catholics should follow the Magisterium of the Church.

Factfile 12 The Virgin Mary

1 "You can't believe in one God and have devotion to the Virgin Mary." Do you agree? Give reasons for your answer, showing you have considered another point of view.

SACRAMENTS

Introduction

Some Christians, such as the Salvation Army and the Society of Friends, do not have sacraments. Most Protestant Christians recognise two sacraments, baptism and the eucharist. The Catholic Church recognises seven sacraments. **Sacraments** are public actions by which Christians receive grace, that is, experience the power and love of God in their lives. The original sacrament for Catholics is Jesus who in his own life showed what God is like. The Church too is a sacrament because it continues to show God's presence in the world. Emphasis on the sacraments is a distinctive feature of Catholic Christianity. The seven sacraments for Catholics represent the high points of their life and are closely related to the liturgy, the public worship of the Church

> The seven sacraments are:
> * Baptism
> * Confirmation
> * The Eucharist
> * Penance and reconciliation
> * Anointing of the sick
> * Holy Orders
>   (see factfiles 45, 46)
> * Matrimony
>   (see factfile 34).

Baptism

Baptism comes from a Greek word meaning bathed or totally washed. Baptism is the sacrament by which a person becomes a member of the Church. It is the religious ceremony of initiation into the Christian community. The origin of baptism for Christians is the baptism of Jesus. It marked a new beginning in his life. God declared him to be his Son and he received the Holy Spirit. A person who is baptised becomes a child of God through the gift of the Holy Spirit. For Catholics baptism is the normal way by which a person becomes a Christian. An early problem for Christians was whether a baby could be baptised or only adults. The majority view was that children can be baptised at the request of their parents. This means that children have to decide as they grow up whether to accept the Christian faith expressed for them at their baptism. Some Christians, particularly the Baptists, do not allow baptism until a person is mature enough to accept it as an expression of personal faith.

The ceremony of baptism

The child of Catholic parents is usually brought to the church for baptism in the first weeks of life. The parents are joined by godparents who must also be Catholics and together they promise to bring the child up in the practice of the faith. Before the child is baptised they renounce sin. They then profess their belief in God the Father, in Jesus Christ, his only Son, and in the Holy Spirit. These statements are a form of the Creed. They are called the baptismal vows and are made on behalf of the child. The priest then baptises the child by pouring water on the head three times. He uses the trinitarian formula, "I baptise you

FACTFILE 13

SACRAMENTS OF INITIATION

Christ instituted the sacraments of the new law. There are seven: Baptism, Confirmation (or Chrismation), the Eucharist, Penance, the Anointing of the Sick, Holy Orders, and Matrimony. The seven sacraments touch all the stages and all the important moments of Christian life: they give birth and increase, healing and mission to the Christian's life of faith. There is thus a certain resemblance between the stages of natural life and the stages of the spiritual life.

Catechism of the Catholic Church (1210).

> ... We have died to sin; how could we go on living in it? You cannot have forgotten that all of us, when we were baptised into Christ Jesus, were baptised into his death. So by our baptism into his death we were buried with him, so that as Christ was raised from the dead by the Father's glorious power, we too should begin living a new life.

Romans 6:2-4.

in the name of the Father, and of the Son, and of the Holy Spirit." Then the child is anointed with **chrism** (consecrated oil). A candle is lit and given to someone from the child's family. This symbolises that the child has received the light of Christ. The ceremony usually takes place at Sunday Mass so that the congregation can welcome the child into the life of the Church.

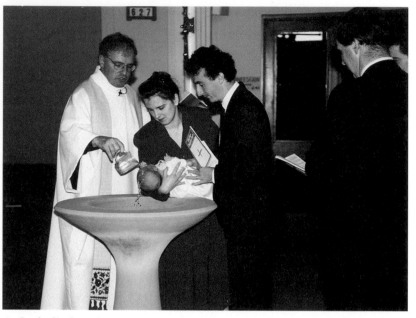

A Catholic baptism.

> Holy Baptism is the basis of the whole Christian life, the gateway to life in the Spirit ... and the door which gives access to the other sacraments. Through Baptism we are freed from sin and reborn as sons of God; we become members of Christ, are incorporated into the Church and made sharers in her mission: 'Baptism is the sacrament of regeneration through water in the word.'

Catechism of the Catholic Church (1213).

Confirmation

Confirmation is also a sacrament of initiation. For many Christians it is an opportunity to confirm actively what was done on their behalf as babies in baptism. The sacrament of confirmation is particularly related to the gift of the Holy Spirit and is usually administered by the bishop rather than the priest. The bishop completes, or confirms, the process of initiation into Christianity begun at baptism. About 100 years ago the practice was for the newly confirmed person to receive communion for the first time. This remains the practice in the Church of England. In 1910 Catholics made a change, allowing children to make their first confession and communion at about the age of seven, and to be confirmed from about the age of ten. There have been attempts since Vatican II to return to the original sequence. Unbaptised adults who become Catholics are expected to receive baptism, confirmation and the eucharist at the same time, preferably during the Easter Vigil.

The ceremony of confirmation

As most children are baptised as babies the sacrament of
confirmation is an opportunity for them when they are older to
make their baptismal vows for themselves. Confirmation
happens less often than baptism. It is given by the bishop who
comes to the church for this purpose. Those to be confirmed
will have been prepared to ensure that they are ready for
confirmation. The ceremony takes place during Mass after the
reading of the Gospel. The bishop explains the meaning of
confirmation and then those about to be confirmed renew their
baptismal vows. He prays for them and asks God to send his
Holy Spirit on them to guide them in the Christian way of life.
Each comes forward and is anointed by the bishop with chrism.
He makes the sign of the cross in chrism on each one's forehead
and says, "Be sealed with the gift of the Holy Spirit." The Mass
then continues but at the end there is a special blessing. Those
who have been confirmed have now completed their initiation
as Catholics into the Christian faith.

In the Roman Rite the bishop extends his hands over the
whole group of the confirmands. Since the time of the
apostles this gesture has signified the gift of the Spirit. The
bishop invokes the pouring of the Spirit in these words:

All-powerful God, Father of our Lord Jesus Christ,
by water and the Holy Spirit you freed your sons and
daughters from sin and gave them new life. Send your Holy
Spirit upon them to be their helper and guide. Give them
the spirit of wisdom and understanding, the spirit of right
judgement and courage, the spirit of knowledge and
reverence. Fill them with the spirit of wonder and awe in
your presence. We ask this through Christ our Lord.

Catechism of the Catholic Church (1299).

FACTFILE 14

THE MASS

Christ Jesus, who died, yes, who was raised from the dead, who is at the right hand of God, who indeed intercedes for us, is present in many ways to his Church: in his word, in his Church's prayer, 'where two or three are gathered in my name,' in the poor, the sick, and the imprisoned, in the sacraments of which he is the author, in the sacrifice of the Mass, and in the person of the minister. But 'he is present ... most *especially in the Eucharistic species.'*

Catechism of the Catholic Church (1373).

Catholics arriving for Mass dip their fingers in the holy water and make the sign of the cross.

Introduction

The Christian practice of dividing days into weeks is an inheritance from Judaism. For Jews each period of seven days ended with the Sabbath, a day of rest and worship. The Gospels state that Jesus died on the day before the Sabbath, on what is now Friday. His body lay in the tomb on the Sabbath (Saturday). The women discovered that he had risen very early on the morning of the first day of the week, that is Sunday. Because of the importance of the resurrection the first day became known as the Lord's Day and the preferred day for weekly worship. Christians gathered together for readings, prayers and instruction and to receive the Eucharist. Catholics continue this practice today by going to Sunday Mass. Protestants also attend church on Sunday but their tradition often puts more emphasis on hymns, readings, prayers and the sermon than on the Eucharist.

The Mass in Catholic life

For most Catholics, going to Mass and receiving communion are at the centre of their life as Christians. The Mass combines the Liturgy of the Word and the Liturgy of the Eucharist. Catholics are obliged to go to Mass every Sunday and on Holy Days of obligation. It is the means by which they express their communal life in the church. They hear the word of God in readings from the Bible, they pray together and they receive the Eucharist. Sunday Mass is a weekly renewal of their faith and vocation as Christians and a celebration of Jesus' resurrection. It reminds them of God's love and of their duty to show God's love in their lives.

Preparations for the Mass

Catholics believe that in order to participate fully in the Mass and receive Holy Communion, they should first be purified from sin. A Catholic who has sinned gravely or mortally should first go to confession and receive God's forgiveness. All present at Mass participate in the 'penitential rite' at the beginning of Mass which purifies all from lesser or venial sins.

Most Catholics make the sign of the cross with holy water when they enter the Church for Mass. Some Catholics also prepare for Mass by using the prayers for the examination of conscience in *The Sunday Missal*.

The structure of the Mass

All present make the sign of the cross, and the celebrant (the presiding priest) greets the people.

The Penitential Rite

The congregation confess that they have sinned and ask for God's forgiveness. The priest then gives absolution.

The Liturgy of the Word

This contains three readings from the Old and New Testaments (including a Gospel reading). These readings are taken from a lectionary based on a three year cycle to cover the Gospels (*Matthew*, *Mark*, *Luke* and *John*). A sermon (homily) on the readings follows, then recitation of the creed and prayers of intercession.

The Liturgy of the Eucharist

The people's gifts and the bread and wine are brought to the altar symbolising the sacrifice of the Mass as a sacrifice of the people as well as God's sacrifice of himself. After the celebrant has washed his hands he says the Eucharistic prayer, joining the sacrifice of the people to the sacrifice of Christ renewed in the Mass. The prayer of consecration follows, and the priest repeats the words of Jesus at the Last Supper which change the whole substance of bread and wine into the body and blood of Jesus. (A bell is usually rung at this point to mark the change of the bread and wine.) All join in the memorial acclamation which highlights what is remembered in the mystery of the Mass. The priest continues the Eucharistic prayer.

Rite of Communion

The people then say the Lord's Prayer to pray for daily food (in both the spiritual and material sense) and forgiveness. Before sharing holy communion, they give each other a sign of peace to show their love for one another and pray for peace and unity. The priest then receives holy communion, and distributes it to the people. Any remaining consecrated hosts are placed in the tabernacle.

Concluding Rite

Finally, the priest blesses the people and ends the Mass by sending them out into the world in the peace brought by the Mass.

The importance of the Mass to Catholics

The Mass is important to Catholics because they believe it is the means of regenerating their lives. The *Catechism* says that Catholics 'receive in the Eucharist the food of eternal life' (*1211*). It is called 'The Holy Mass because the liturgy in which the mystery of salvation is accomplished concludes with the sending forth (*missio*) of the faithful, so that they may fulfil God's will in their daily lives.' (*1332.*)

The Mass is a sacrifice:
- the sacrifice of the people is seen in the offering of gifts and bread and wine and in the commitment of their lives;
- the sacrifice of Christ is renewed on the altar and offered by the Church to the Father. The faithful are nourished on the body and blood of Jesus.

> In the Eucharist Christ gives us the very body which he gave up for us on the cross, the very blood which he 'poured out for many for the forgiveness of sins'. The Eucharist is thus a sacrifice because it re-presents (makes present) the sacrifice of the cross ...

Catechism of the Catholic Church (1365-1366).

The Mass is a communion:
- it unites the faithful with Christ and it unites them with each other through the sharing of bread and giving the sign of peace.

> By the consecration of the bread and wine there takes place a change of the whole substance of the bread into the substance of the body of Christ our Lord and of the whole substance of the wine into the substance of his blood. This change the holy Catholic Church has fittingly and properly called transubstantiation.

Catechism of the Catholic Church (1376).

Greeting one another with the sign of peace.

> Almighty God, we pray that your angel may take this sacrifice to your altar in heaven. Then as we receive from this altar the sacred body and blood of your Son, let us be filled with every grace and blessing.

Eucharistic Prayer, The Sunday Missal.

FACTFILE 15

THE EUCHARIST

Eucharist comes from the Greek word meaning 'thanksgiving' and is the correct technical term for what Catholics usually refer to as holy communion. It is a ritual meal to celebrate and renew all that God has done through the death and resurrection of Jesus. This sacrament gives thanks as Jesus did to God before he gave the bread and wine to his disciples. He used the bread to show that his body would be broken and the wine to show that his blood would be shed. The giving of his body is Jesus giving up his life and the shedding of his blood is his covenant with God. The relationship between God and human beings, which started in the Old Testament, is completed by the death and resurrection of Jesus. This is the mystery of faith which the Eucharist expresses and proclaims.

Holy Communion

Communion comes from the Latin word meaning sharing. Originally Christians shared one loaf which they all ate and one cup from which they all drank. This sharing of food represents the sharing of life. People in a family, close friends, members of a community, share food together. Christians regard themselves as members of God's family and so they eat God's food together.

It represents the spiritual nourishment and development they receive. Catholics emphasise holy communion more than other Christians. Non-Catholic Christians are not allowed to receive holy communion unless they are members of a Church which is in communion with the Catholic Church because sharing in communion is seen as a sign of full communion between Christians.

The Lord's Supper

Many Protestants refer to the Eucharist as the Lord's Supper. This expression emphasises that it is a meal and that it is eaten in memory of Jesus. It is also a reminder of the Last Supper which Jesus had with the twelve apostles on the night before he died. The Eucharistic Prayer said by the priest in the Mass, contains the words from the Gospels and Paul put together in one version. The words and actions of Jesus with the bread and wine are referred to as the institution of the Eucharist. Food had always been important in the Jewish religion and there was a belief that when the Messiah came there would be a great feast. This would satisfy people's spiritual longings as well as their physical hunger. Christians regard the Eucharist as a spiritual feast.

On the night he was betrayed, he took bread and gave you thanks and praise. He broke the bread, gave it to his disciples, and said:
'Take this, all of you, and eat it: this is my body which will be given up for you.'

When supper was ended, he took the cup. Again he gave you thanks and praise, gave the cup to his disciples, and said:
'Take this, all of you, and drink from it: this is the cup of my blood, the blood of the new and everlasting covenant. It will be shed for you and for all so that sins may be forgiven. Do this in memory of me.'

At the Last Supper, on the night he was betrayed, our Saviour instituted the Eucharistic sacrifice of his Body and Blood. This he did in order to perpetuate the sacrifice of the cross throughout the ages until he should come again, and so to entrust to his beloved Spouse, the Church, a memorial of his death and resurrection: a sacrament of love, a sign of unity, a bond of charity, a Paschal banquet 'in which Christ is consumed, the mind is filled with grace, and a pledge of future glory is given to us.'

Catechism of the Catholic Church (1323).

Eucharistic Prayer, The Sunday Missal.

'The Last Supper' by Juan de Juanes.

The breaking of bread

It was the custom in the time of Jesus to break a loaf with the hands rather than slice it with a knife. The nourishment of the bread cannot be received unless the bread is broken. Just as a father or mother would break the loaf for children so Jesus would do the same for his disciples. By a simple everyday action which Jesus did for the last time before his death he used words to connect the bread with his body. Protestants use the expression 'the breaking of bread' because it is the one used in the New Testament. It also suggests an ordinary but symbolic action rather than a sacramental event renewing the sacrifice of Jesus. In the Catholic Church small wafers of unleavened bread are used. Many Protestants break up a small loaf. Catholics drink the wine from the same cup or cups but Protestants often use small individual cups. Some Protestants use unfermented grape juice so that no one is made to consume alcohol.

The real presence

The Real Presence refers to the belief that Jesus is really present in the Eucharist. At the time of the Reformation this was a major issue dividing Catholics and Protestants. Catholic belief is that at the moment of consecration the bread ceases to be bread and becomes the body of Jesus, and the wine ceases to be wine and becomes his blood. This is explained by the doctrine of **transubstantiation** – the substance of the bread and wine had changed although they appeared to remain the same. Some Catholics today are exploring new ways of speaking about the real presence of Jesus in this sacrament, under the appearances of bread and wine. Jesus is really present under the appearances of bread and the wine, not literally or physically, but as a sacrament. Most Protestants believe that the Eucharist is a sacrament in which the bread and wine are symbols of the presence of Jesus. Catholics and Protestants agree that Jesus is present to Christians through the sacrament of the Eucharist, though they have different understandings of how.

Receiving communion.

Penance and reconciliation (confession)

This is the more familiar of the two sacraments of healing. It is also called the sacrament of penance or confession because in its best known form Catholics confess their sins to a priest. The sacrament requires three acts from the penitent: **contrition** – sorrow for the sin committed and the resolution not to sin again; **confession** – admission of responsibility, to the representative of the Church; and **satisfaction** – compensation to the person who has been wronged and the willingness to do penance to restore the relationship with God. The priest pronounces **absolution** and imposes an act of **penance**. This sacrament reconciles people with God and with each other. It can bring peace to a troubled conscience and give strength to avoid repeating past sins in the future. The sacrament of reconciliation is a reminder that Christians enjoy the love of God by living in accordance with his will and under his judgement.

Anointing of the sick

This is the other sacrament of healing and is for those who are in danger of death from illness or old age. It is given by a priest who anoints the person on the forehead and hands with **chrism** (consecrated oil). This sacrament may be received whenever a person falls ill or the illness worsens. Its purpose is to give spiritual strength and healing to the whole person, including restoration to health, if such is God's will. It is a reminder of, and an opportunity to share in, the suffering of Jesus before his death. It unites a person with the whole Christian community, past and present. It may mark the end of a person's life on earth and the preparation for the final part of the journey. In addition to the anointing of the sick, a dying person, if fit to receive it, may be given the Eucharist for the last time. This last communion is called **viaticum** which means food, literally for the journey. These practices reflect in sacramental form the concern and compassion of Jesus expressed in the Gospels.

SACRAMENTS OF HEALING

Making confession to a priest.

Illness and suffering have always been among the gravest problems confronted in human life. In illness, man experiences his powerlessness, his limitations, and his finitude. Every illness can make us glimpse death.

Illness can lead to anguish, self-absorption, sometimes even despair and revolt against God. It can also make a person more mature, helping him discern in his life what is not essential so that he can turn toward that which is. Very often illness provokes a search for God and a return to him.

Catechism of the Catholic Church (1500-01).

QUESTIONS

Factfile 13 Sacraments of Initiation

1 Give a definition of baptism.

2 Why do Catholics have their children baptised?

3 What are the main features of a baptism ceremony?

4 Why are Catholics confirmed?

Factfile 14 The Mass

1 Why is Sunday the day of worship for Christians?

2 Explain what is meant by:
   (a) the Liturgy of the Word;
   (b) the Liturgy of the Eucharist.

3 Why is the Mass important to Catholics?

Factfile 15 The Eucharist

1 What is the Eucharist a thanksgiving for?

2 Why is the Eucharist called the Lord's Supper?

3 What are the bread and wine?

4 "You don't need symbols to feel God's presence." Do you agree? Give reasons for your answer, showing that you have considered another point of view.

Factfile 16 Sacraments of Healing

1 Name three acts of the penitent.

2 Why is the sacrament of penance known mainly as the sacrament of reconciliation?

3 What is the purpose of the sacrament of anointing of the sick?

4 What is *viaticum*?

PUBLIC WORSHIP

Public worship is the phrase used to describe how religious believers join together to praise and thank God and deepen their faith in him. In Christianity it can take several forms, and many acts of public worship will contain more than one form.

1 Liturgical worship

This worship follows a written order of service. The leader of worship often wears special clothes and uses set actions. A typical liturgical service is the Catholic Mass, with the priest using set words, wearing special vestments and performing set actions such as the elevation of the host.

Protestant Churches also have liturgical services (mainly for the Eucharist). The Church of England's services of Mattins and Evensong (morning and evening prayer) are also liturgical worship.

FACTFILE 17

DIFFERENT FORMS OF WORSHIP

The priest invites the people to call to mind their sins, and to repent of them. He may use the following or similar words:
'My brothers and sisters, to prepare ourselves to celebrate the sacred mysteries, let us call to mind our sins.'
A pause for silent reflection follows. After the silence, one of ... three forms of the penitential rite is chosen (for example):
'I confess to almighty God and to you, my brothers and sisters, that I have sinned through my own fault. (All strike their breast.) In my thoughts and in my words, in what I have done, and in what I have failed to do; and I ask blessed Mary, ever virgin, and all the angels and saints, and you, my brothers and sisters, to pray for me to the Lord our God.'

Extract from The Sunday Missal showing the set order, words and actions of liturgical worship.

2 Non-liturgical worship

This worship has no set prayers or actions, and sometimes, no special vestments for the leader. A typical non-liturgical service is a Nonconformist Sunday service. It consists of hymns, extempore prayers (impromptu, rather than set prayers), Bible readings and a sermon preached on one of the Bible readings. Such worship usually follows a regular pattern and usually the Bible readings follow a lectionary.

Pentecost (Whitsunday)
Morning   Evening
Joel 2:23-29 (or 21-32)   *Exodus* 19:16-25
Acts 2:1-11   *Acts* 4:23-27
John 14:15-27

Extract from lectionary, Methodist Service Book.

3 Spontaneous (charismatic) worship

This worship has no set form. The leader acts as he feels inspired by the Holy Spirit. A typical spontaneous service would be a Pentecostal service. It might include speaking in tongues, healings, Bible readings, a sermon, Gospel hymns, and testimonies. In White Churches the leader does not wear special clothes, but many Black Churches have a robed choir and a minister in vestments.

All Christian worship includes praise, thanksgiving, intercession (asking God's help for others), Bible readings and a sermon.

FACTFILE 18

TITLES AND ORIGINS OF THE EUCHARIST

The *Catechism of the Catholic Church (1328-1332)* gives over ten titles for this sacrament, including:

Eucharist means 'thanksgiving' and is the word used by all Christians to describe what most Catholics call the Mass. When Jesus broke bread with his disciples, he 'gave thanks' and this service is the main public thanksgiving of Christians.

Mass is thought to come from the Latin *'missa'* meaning 'send out', perhaps referring to the way in which the Mass gives Catholics the power of Christ with which the priest sends them out into the world.

The Holy Sacrifice refers to the one sacrifice of Christ the Saviour and includes the offering of the Church.

Holy Communion is a title more widely used than Eucharist. It refers to the way in which the Eucharist gives special communion or participation between Christ and the communicants and unites the communicants with each other. Catholics use it to refer especially to the sharing of the bread and wine.

Lord's Supper is used to emphasise the way in which the Eucharist commemorates Jesus' (the Lord's) last supper with his disciples. This title is used by those who believe the Eucharist is only a remembrance of what happened at the Last Supper and by St Paul in the New Testament.

Breaking of Bread refers to the central act of the Eucharist where Jesus broke bread and shared it with his disciples. It is especially used by Christians who use ordinary bread rather than wafers for the Eucharist.

The **origins of the Eucharist** are found in the New Testament, in the life of Jesus and in the actions of the early Christians. The Eucharist was begun by Jesus at the Last Supper. It is described in *Mark 14:22-24.*

> And as they were eating he took bread, and when he had said the blessing he broke it and gave it to them. "Take it," he said, "this is my body." Then he took a cup, and when he had given thanks he handed it to them, and all drank from it, and he said to them "This is my blood, the blood of the covenant, poured out for many."

Mark 14:22-24.

Soon after Jesus' death Christian worship included a remembrance of this act:

> Each day, with one heart, they regularly went to the Temple but met in their houses for the breaking of bread; they shared their food gladly and generously; they praised God and were looked up to by everyone. Day by day the Lord added to their community those destined to be saved.

Acts 2:46-47.

Only fifteen years after Jesus' death, Paul had to write to the Christians in Corinth about the proper way to celebrate the Lord's Supper, indicating its importance in Christian worship:

> For the tradition I received from the Lord and also handed on to you is that on the night he was betrayed, the Lord Jesus took some bread, and after he had given thanks, he broke it, and he said, "This is my body, which is for you; do this in remembrance of me." And in the same way, with the cup after supper, saying, "This cup is the new covenant in my blood. Whenever you drink it, do this as a memorial of me." Whenever you eat this bread, then, and drink this cup, you are proclaiming the Lord's death until he comes.

1 Corinthians 11: 23-26.

It was above all on 'the first day of the week', Sunday, the day of Jesus' resurrection, that the Christians met to 'break bread'. From that time on down to our own day the celebration of the Eucharist has been continued so that today we encounter it everywhere in the Church with the same fundamental structure. It remains the centre of the Church's life.

Catechism of the Catholic Church (1343).

The window in the Blessed Sacrament Chapel at Buckfast Abbey.

THE EUCHARIST IN OTHER CHRISTIAN TRADITIONS

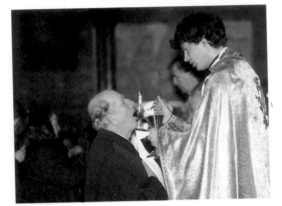

In the Orthodox Churches, the bread is dipped into the wine and people receive communion on a spoon.

Catholic Eucharist

See factfiles 14 and 15.

Orthodox Eucharist

The Orthodox Churches call the Eucharist 'The Liturgy'.

PRACTICES

1 The Preparation

Before the public liturgy, the priests and deacons meet in a special area to prepare themselves and the bread and wine. The bread is an ordinary loaf often given by a member of the congregation. Some of this bread is broken off and placed on the paten. Any remaining bread is given to the congregation after the service to take home. The wine is placed in a chalice and then the bread and wine are covered with a veil and incense is wafted over them. Many set prayers accompany these actions.

2 The Liturgy of the Word

The Gospel is brought from the sanctuary through the doors of the iconostasis by the priest with acolytes carrying candles. It is then read and sometimes a sermon is given. The Gospel is taken back through the iconostasis and replaced on the altar. More prayers are said.

3 The Eucharist

The altar, church and congregation are censed to prepare them. Then the priests and deacons bring the chalice and paten from the place of preparation, through the door of the iconostasis into the congregation, then back through the other door and placed on the altar. The congregation prepares for the Eucharist by confessing their sins and, at certain times of the year, prostrating themselves on the floor.

The priest says several Eucharistic prayers, especially the *epiklesis* prayer, which calls on God the Father to send the Holy Spirit to enter the bread and wine and change them into the body and blood of Jesus. The bread is then broken and elevated and the people are blessed by the priest. The priests take their communion, then the bread is placed in the wine, brought through the iconostasis and given to the people on a spoon.

The priest then blesses and dismisses the congregation, usually with a dimissal anthem. Any remaining consecrated bread is placed in the tabernacle.

BELIEFS

The liturgy symbolises the belief that God is separate from the world (the altar area represents God divided from the people by the iconostasis and the bridge between the world and God is Jesus (represented by the priests).

The people must be made holy to receive Christ in the bread and wine which mysteriously change into the body and blood of Christ.

The Orthodox Eucharist celebrates the ordinary becoming holy: God coming into people's everyday lives.

Protestant Worship

Although some Protestant Churches celebrate the Eucharist only once a month, others, such as the Anglican Church (Church of England) and the Brethren, have a weekly Eucharist. There is a great variety of forms of worship within the Anglican Church. Some churches have a form of service that is similar to the Catholic Mass while others follow a more Protestant non-sacramental form of worship. Here are the main features of Protestant Eucharists based on the *Methodist Service Book*.

PRACTICES
1 The Preparation
All the people confess their sins and there are hymns and prayers of praise.

2 The Ministry of the Word
There are three Bible readings (usually from a lectionary) with a sermon followed by another hymn and prayers of intercession for the Church and the world.

3 The Lord's Supper
The peace is shared around the Church. Everyone says the creed.

There is another hymn and then the bread and wine are either brought to the communion table or uncovered if they have been placed there before the service. The bread is ordinary bread, sometimes cut up, the wine is in small separate glasses and is often non-alcoholic.

The minister says the Eucharistic Prayer, with the words of institution, and then breaks the bread. The people say, 'Though we are many, we are one body because we all share in the one loaf.' In the communion the minister gives the bread with words including 'in remembrance that Christ died for you' and 'feed on him in your hearts'. Often the bread and wine are given out and everyone eats and drinks at the same time.

4 The Final Prayers
There is a prayer of thanks to God for the sacrament and a dismissal of the people to go out into the world with greater power to be good Christians.

BELIEFS
Protestant holy communion makes the common things of life holy, but there is no mystery. Protestants believe nothing happens to the bread and wine – they are only symbols of Christ's presence in people's hearts.

The communion unites Christians with each other and with Christ and increases their spiritual awareness.

> As we eat and drink these holy gifts in the presence of your divine majesty, fill us with your grace and heavenly blessing; nourish us with the body and blood of your Son, that we may grow into his likeness.

Eucharistic Prayer, Church of England Alternative Service Book.

Christians who do not celebrate the Eucharist

Liturgical worship is often called 'altar worship' because of its close connection with the Eucharist. Quakers (members of the Society of Friends) and Salvationists (members of the Salvation Army) do not have any form of altar worship and do not celebrate the Eucharist.

Quaker worship concentrates on 'waiting on the Spirit'. A normal Quaker service may have readings and prayers and people sharing their thoughts with each other and God as they wait for some form of response from God. It may be completely silent.

Salvationist worship centres on the Bible, hymns and personal experience of God's presence in **testimonies** (telling the congregation how Christ has changed your life) and conversion. Quakers and Salvationists reject sacraments because:

- They believe every Christian is ordained a priest by the Spirit. Therefore, they cannot accept services where one person is made more important than the rest. Most Protestants accept the idea known as 'the priesthood of all believers'. In other words, everyone is called to be a priest.

- They believe that rituals cannot change the nature of things.

- Quakers believe Jesus wanted every Christian meal to be a remembrance of the Last Supper, so they remember Jesus every time they eat and drink.

- Both groups believe that the New Covenant of Jesus removed the need for ceremonial because Jesus is the only priest we need.

- Salvationists will have nothing to do with alcohol. They spend much of the time helping down-and-outs and the homeless, many of whose lives have been ruined by alcohol.

- Both groups believe that worship should be a direct personal relationship with God which needs no symbols like bread and wine.

W e believe that Jesus is really present in our worship, and that the whole of our lives are receptive to the action of God in them ... The lack of symbols is itself a symbol, that you go to God direct, without need of anything in between.'

Janet Scott, a Quaker, in 'Christians in Britain Today'.

The Friends Meeting House, New Earswick, York. Everyone at the meeting is considered equal, but elders, who sit in the meeting, bring it to a close by shaking hands, the clerk reading out any notices. Children often attend the meeting for worship for only about ten minutes, since it is considered too long for them to sit in silence for the whole time. They are looked after in another room.

Exterior features

Many Church of England churches had a graveyard and lych-gate (where the coffin rested on its way from the unholy material world to the holy world of the Church) and a tower or spire with bells.

Roman Catholic churches had a crucifix and/or statues of the Virgin Mary and saints outside the Church.

Protestant Nonconformist churches were very plain with a noticeboard outside with verses from the Bible or some 'wayside pulpit' giving a Christian message to passers-by.

Although some older churches still have these features, modern churches tend to look very similar from the outside regardless of their denomination. Many Orthodox churches and some Pentecostal churches have taken over redundant Anglican or Nonconformist churches and can only be identified from their interior features.

St Mary's Cathedral, Middlesbrough.

Interior features

All Catholic churches will have:
- **a crucifix**
- **an altar with candles**
- **a tabernacle with reserved sacrament**
- **a font**
- **Stations of the Cross**
- **a statue of the Blessed Virgin Mary**.

The crucifix, altar and tabernacle demonstrate belief in the Eucharist as a sacrifice and the transformation of the bread and wine into the body and blood of Jesus. Visual symbols are important so a crucifix is used rather than a cross to show it is the sacrifice of Jesus which forgives our sins. This belief is also illustrated in the Stations of the Cross.

A lych-gate.

A statue of the Virgin Mary outside a Catholic church.

The font shows the belief in infant baptism as there is no room for full immersion.

All Catholic Churches have a statue of the Blessed Virgin Mary. Catholics believe that Mary is the Mother of God and is also a perfect example for Christians to follow. Prayers are offered to Mary who can intercede for people with God.

Candles are lit on the altar or by individual worshippers at the back of the Church, often in front of statues. Catholics see God as the light of the world. Incense is often used. The symbol of rising smoke, dating back to the Old Testament, represents our prayers rising to God.

The altar in St Mary's Cathedral, Middlesbrough.

All Orthodox churches will have:
- **an altar with a crucifix and candles**
- **a tabernacle with reserved sacrament**
- **an iconostasis with icons of Jesus, Mary and the saints separating the people from the altar**
- **icons with candles in front of them**
- **no pews.**

The altar with a crucifix and candles shows the Orthodox belief that the bread and wine become the body and blood of Christ.

The iconostasis shows the Orthodox belief in the separation of earth and heaven, that heaven came to earth in Jesus and that part of heaven is the sanctuary which can only be bridged by priests.

Orthodox Christians have special religious paintings of Mary, Jesus and the saints (called **icons**) instead of statues. These show their belief in praying to God through Mary and the saints, the continuity of Christians and the idea that all Christians are part of one family.

There are no pews because Orthodox Christians believe that people should be free to move about in worship, especially to prostrate themselves (kneel and put their foreheads onto the ground).

An iconostasis.

All Protestant Churches will have:
- **a communion table**
- **a plain cross**
- **an open Bible on the communion table**
- **a large pulpit**
- **a font or baptismal pool.**

A plain table with no candles symbolises Protestant belief that the Eucharist is only a memorial, there is no change in the bread and wine, no sacrifice and no need for a priest.

A plain cross is a sign that there should be no images in worship – no statues, icons, or candles for individuals to light – prayer should be offered directly to God through Jesus.

Protestants believe that God communicates with humans through the Bible. The central part of worship is to listen to the Bible and to have it related to life today in a sermon.

Most Protestant churches have a small font symbolising belief in infant baptism, but some (all Baptist and some Pentecostal churches) have a baptismal pool symbolising belief in believers' baptism (adult baptism).

A communion table in a Protestant church.

QUESTIONS

Factfile 17 Different Forms of Worship

1 What are the differences between liturgical and non-liturgical worship?

2 What are the differences between liturgical and spontaneous worship?

Factfile 18 Titles and Origins of the Eucharist

1 What are five alternative titles for the Mass?

2 What two events is the Mass based on?

Factfile 19 The Eucharist in Other Christian Traditions

1 Describe the similar features in Catholic, Orthodox and Protestant Eucharists.

2 What things do Orthodox and Protestants do at Eucharist that Catholics do not?

3 Why do some Christians not celebrate the Eucharist?

4 "You don't need religious rituals to worship God." Do you agree? Give reasons for your answer, showing you have considered another point of view.

Factfile 20 Places of Worship

1 Why do different churches have different features?

⑥ FESTIVALS AND PILGRIMAGE

Advent

Biblical background

Advent is the season of preparation for Christmas. For the four Sundays before Christmas, Catholics are encouraged to think about the coming of Jesus. Readings from the Old Testament are used to show how God prepared for the coming of Jesus. Many of the New Testament readings describe the second coming of Jesus and the judgement we will face when he comes again.

How it is celebrated

In many churches there is an advent crown or ring with four candles round the outside for the four Sundays before Christmas and a candle in the middle for Christmas Day. Each candle symbolises one of the events to reflect on in Advent – God's Word in the Bible, the prophets, John the Baptist, the Virgin Mary, and finally, on Christmas Day, a candle is lit for Jesus, the light of the world. Many of the celebrations in Advent are connected with the claim in *John* 1:18 that Jesus is the light of the world.

Each Sunday Mass in Advent has special readings and prayers to prepare people for Christmas. There are special advent hymns.

The meaning of Advent

Christians believe that Advent is a time to think about what the coming of Jesus means. They prepare in their hearts not just to remember the coming of Jesus at the first Christmas, but also to examine their lives to make sure they are ready for Christ's return.

In the Orthodox Church Advent is a time of penitence and they prepare for Christmas with a forty day fast.

> Let all mortal flesh keep silence
> And with fear and trembling stand;
> Ponder nothing earthly-minded,
> For with blessing in his hand
> Christ our God to earth descendeth,
> Our full homage to demand.

Ancient Advent hymn.

ADVENT AND CHRISTMAS

An advent crown.

Christmas

Biblical background

The celebration of Christmas is based on the nativity stories in *Matthew* 1 and 2 and *Luke* 1 and 2.

Matthew records that Mary and Joseph were betrothed (legally engaged to be married) when Joseph discovered Mary was pregnant. He wanted to stop the wedding plans because he had not had sex with Mary. An angel appeared to him and told him the child she was expecting was God's son who would save the world from sin as God had promised in the Old Testament. So Joseph went ahead and married Mary anyway. Jesus was born in Bethlehem and was visited by wise men from the East who had seen the birth of the Messiah forecast in the stars. God warned Joseph that King Herod wanted to kill Jesus and so Joseph took Mary and Jesus to Egypt. After Herod's death, they went to live in Nazareth.

Luke records that Jesus was the cousin of John the Baptist. John was born to Elizabeth and Zachariah when they were old and Zachariah was told that John would be God's messenger. Luke states that Mary was visited by the angel Gabriel when she was betrothed to Joseph. He told her that she would conceive and bear a son, Jesus the Messiah, and the child would come from God. Gabriel told Mary about Elizabeth and Mary went to visit her. When she went in John the Baptist leapt in his mother's womb and Elizabeth knew Mary was special – 'Blessed are you among women and blessed is the fruit of your womb' she said to Mary. Mary responded to this news by saying the Magnificat ('My soul magnifies the Lord ...' *Luke* 1:46-55).
Mary returned to Nazareth, but she and Joseph had to go to Bethlehem. The Emperor Augustus had ordered a census and everyone had to return to the town of their birth. Jesus was born in a stable there because there was no room in the inn. After his birth angels appeared to shepherds in the fields outside Bethlehem and told them about the birth of their saviour Jesus. The shepherds rushed to the stable and told Mary and Joseph about the angels' message. After eight days Jesus was circumcised, then taken to Jerusalem to be presented at the Temple as the Old Testament Law requires. At the Temple an old priest, Simeon, and an old prophetess, Anna, recognised Jesus as the saviour promised by God. Mary and Joseph returned to Nazareth where Jesus was brought up.

How it is celebrated

Christmas is celebrated by trees, lights, exchanging presents, sending cards and feasting. All of these are ways for Christians to celebrate God's greatest gift to humans, his son. So they give gifts or cards and remember in the trees and lights the life and light Jesus brought.

Catholics celebrate with a vigil Mass on the afternoon of Christmas Eve where they prepare for Christmas. It is a special service with special readings and responses to remember the meaning of Christmas. There are three Christmas Masses: Midnight Mass on Christmas Eve, where the crib is often set up and blessed;. Mass at dawn; and another Mass later in the day. These three Masses remember all the events of Christmas

Lord as we keep tonight the vigil of Christmas may we celebrate this Eucharist with greater joy than ever since it marks the beginning of our redemption.

From the vigil Mass of Christmas, The Sunday Missal.

recorded in the Gospels and give people an opportunity to celebrate the coming of Jesus into the world.

On the Sunday after Christmas there is a special Mass for the Holy Family (Jesus, Mary and Joseph) where Gospel references to their family life are read and there are special prayers about the perfect example of the holy family and the importance of family life.

There is a special Mass on New Year's Day to remember the importance of the Virgin Mary in the birth and upbringing of Jesus.

The meaning of Christmas

Catholics believe that Christmas celebrates the great turning point in human history. Before the birth of Jesus, it was only possible to have a partial relationship with God. Christians believe that God was born as man in Jesus. This is called **incarnation**. Jesus' life, death and resurrection means that sins have been forgiven so it has become possible for humans to have a full relationship with God and go to heaven after death.

Epiphany

Literally, **epiphany** means 'made known'. It is the festival when Christians remember the way Jesus was made known to the people of his time. It is celebrated on 6 January every year.

Biblical background

Jesus was first made known to the whole world in the coming of the wise men to Bethlehem as recorded in *Matthew 2:1-20*. The wise men represent all the nations who were prophesied in the Old Testament to 'come to the light of God's dawning brightness' (*Isaiah 60:3*). Their gifts of gold (kingship), frankincense (holiness) and myrrh (suffering) not only symbolise the nature of Jesus, but also show how we must respond to his life.

> To become children of God, we must be 'born from above' or 'born of God'. Only when Christ is formed in us will the mystery of Christmas be fulfilled in us. Christmas is the mystery of this marvellous exchange ...

Catechism of the Catholic Church (526).

> The Epiphany is the manifestation of Jesus as Messiah of Israel, Son of God and Saviour of the world. The great feast of Epiphany celebrates the adoration of Jesus by the wise men (magi) from the East, together with his baptism in the Jordan and the wedding feast at Cana in Galilee.

Catechism of the Catholic Church (528).

The three wise men present gifts to Jesus.

How it is celebrated

In the Catholic Church a special Mass is celebrated on the Feast of Epiphany. On the Sunday after Epiphany, there is a Mass remembering the Baptism of Jesus when God opened the heavens and declared that Jesus was his beloved son.

The meaning of Epiphany

Epiphany is a time for remembering that Christ came to bring salvation to the whole world and to think of life as a pilgrimage. Rather like the wise men travelling behind the star, so Christians should travel behind Jesus.

FACTFILE 22

LENT AND HOLY WEEK

At the Ash Wednesday Mass. What is the priest doing here?

Lent

Biblical background

According to Matthew, Mark and Luke, after his baptism Jesus spent 40 days in the wilderness being tempted by the Devil and preparing himself for his ministry.

How it is kept

On Shrove Tuesday people eat pancakes as a reminder of the days when all meat, sugars and fats were eaten up because none of these foods were allowed during Lent. (The Eastern Orthodox Churches still keep such a fast in Lent.)

On Ash Wednesday Catholics go to Church for a special Penitential Mass. As a sign of their penitence they have a cross of ashes smeared on their forehead by the priest. The ashes are made from the leaves blessed at the Palm Sunday Mass the previous year. It is hoped that the cross of ashes will remind people of their Lenten practices of prayer, fasting and almsgiving. Many Catholics give up certain things during Lent. There are also special meetings (sometimes with other local Christians) to prepare for Easter by thinking about the meaning of Easter. Most Christians regard Lent as an opportunity to think about their faith. They devote themselves to God by giving something up, such as smoking, alcohol or sweets.

Holy Week

There are two main celebrations: Palm Sunday which begins Holy Week; and the **Paschal Triduum** which runs from the evening of Maundy Thursday, to the evening of Easter Day.

Biblical background

Palm Sunday is recorded in *Mark* 11 as Jesus' triumphal entry into Jerusalem on an ass. This shows he was the Messiah, but also the suffering servant of God, welcomed by the people who later in the week would call for his crucifixion.

Maundy Thursday is recorded in *Mark* 14. Jesus met with his disciples in an upper room in Jerusalem for a Passover supper. At supper, Jesus set out the pattern for the Eucharist as he blessed and distributed the bread and wine to his disciples. After supper Jesus went to the Garden of Gethsemane to pray about what he knew was going to happen. He asked his disciples to stay awake with him, but they kept falling asleep. During the prayer Jesus accepted that he must follow where God was leading him. After praying, Judas arrived with the High Priest's guards and Jesus was arrested and taken for trial at the High Priest's house. Peter followed, but when he was challenged by the guards about being a follower of Jesus, he denied it three times so fulfilling a prophecy of Jesus.

Good Friday is recorded in *Mark* 15. Jesus was taken by the chief priests to a trial before the Roman Governor, Pontius Pilate. He tried to release him by the custom of releasing a prisoner at Passover, but the chief priests stirred up the people to ask for a rebel leader, Barabbas. The Roman soldiers mocked Jesus and whipped him, then led him to be crucified. An African, Simon of Cyrene, was forced to carry his cross to Golgotha where Jesus was crucified. Passers-by mocked him, asking why he could not save himself when he had saved others. After three hours on the cross, Jesus died. At that moment, the curtain of the Temple was torn in two (symbolising that Jesus' death had broken the division between God and humans). Jesus was taken from the cross and buried in a stone tomb belonging to Joseph of Arimathea who had asked Pilate's permission to take Jesus' body.

Holy Saturday has no biblical record as Jesus was in the tomb.

How it is celebrated
On **Palm Sunday** palm crosses are given out and there may be a procession to the church with the people carrying palm branches. The priest and people make a special entrance into the church, singing hosanna and then the story of the entry into Jerusalem is read from the Gospel. This is followed by a special Mass at which the whole Passion Story (for example *Mark* 14-15) is read.

There is a special evening Mass on **Maundy Thursday** when the bells are rung for the last time before Easter. All the readings are about Jesus' Last Supper with his disciples. These are followed by a footwashing ceremony in which the priest follows the example of Jesus washing his disciples' feet. At the end of Mass, the blessed sacrament is transferred to the tabernacle or other chosen place as there is no Mass on Good Friday and Holy Saturday (as the elements are transferred, not consecrated, it is holy communion). The altar is stripped at the end of the Mass and all crosses removed or covered. The congregation are expected to spend some time at the end of the service in adoration of the blessed sacrament.

Getting ready for a Palm Sunday procession.

The washing of feet, Maundy Thursday.

God our Father, we are gathered here to share in the supper which your only son left to his Church to reveal his love. He gave it to us when he was about to die and commanded us to celebrate it as the new and eternal sacrifice.

Opening Prayer, Maundy Thursday; The Sunday Missal.

On **Good Friday** there is a special service at 3:00 p.m. to remember the crucifixion. It has three parts:

- Liturgy of the Word – Bible readings (especially the whole trial and crucifixion record from John's Gospel) and prayers for the whole world (including Jews and non-believers).
- Veneration of the Cross – the cross is unveiled in three stages either at the altar, or as it is brought to the altar, in solemn procession. The priest and the people then come forward to venerate the cross by a genuflection or a kiss. Special hymns are sung whilst candles are lit around the cross.
- Holy Communion – the Blessed Sacrament is brought from its repository in the *ciborium* and after special prayers is distributed to the people.

Many churches also follow the Stations of the Cross on Good Friday.

The second Station of the Cross.

FACTFILE 23

EASTER AND PENTECOST

Easter Day

Biblical background

According to *Mark* 16, the women followers of Jesus went to the tomb on the Sunday morning to anoint his body for burial. (They could not do so on Good Friday because the Sabbath had started at sunset.) When they arrived, the stone had been rolled away and Jesus' body was gone. A young man in a white robe told them that Jesus was risen and that they were to tell his disciples he had gone ahead of them to Galilee. The other Gospels describe the risen Jesus meeting his disciples in Jerusalem and in Galilee.

How it is celebrated

On **Holy Saturday** night there should be a Vigil in the hours of darkness. In some churches the Vigil takes place just before midnight so that the Mass is celebrated on Easter Day. The Vigil is the first celebration of Easter and has four parts.

1 The Service of Light – the church is in darkness as the priest blesses the fire and lights the Easter candle from the new fire. The Easter candle is then blessed and carried in procession

into the church where everyone lights a candle from the Easter candle and special Easter proclamations and responses are read.

2 Liturgy of the Word – there are nine readings culminating in the Gospel reading of the empty tomb and resurrection.

3 Liturgy of baptism – in some churches there will be baptisms, but in many the service is concerned with the congregation's renewal of their baptismal promises. (This also takes place when there are baptisms.) Water is placed in the font and blessed, the priest reads out the baptismal promises and the people affirm their commitment to them, then they are sprinkled with the holy water.

4 Liturgy of the Eucharist – (even if it takes place before midnight, this is still the first Mass of Easter and the resurrection).

> Father we share in the light of your glory through your Son, the light of the world. Make this new fire holy, and inflame us with new hope. Purify our minds by this Easter celebration, and bring us one day to the feast of eternal light.

The blessing of the fire prayer at the Easter Vigil, The Sunday Missal.

There is a second Easter Mass on Easter Day. This Mass contains special Easter antiphons and responses and can have a repetition of the renewal of baptismal vows.

The Easter candle is lighted from the new fire.

Meaning

The Vigil and Service of Light remind people of Jesus' time in the tomb and the joy and light of the resurrection. The renewal of baptismal vows reminds people of the rebirth which the resurrection of Jesus brings to all believers. The Bible readings remind the people of how God created the world for good and that good creation was brought back to us through the resurrection of Jesus.

All the celebrations remind Catholics that Jesus conquered death and through faith and the sacraments of the Church, they too will conquer death.

For all these reasons, Easter is a time of great joy in the Church.

> Dear friends, through the paschal mystery we have been buried with Christ in baptism, so that we may rise with him to a new life. Now that we have completed our lenten observance, let us renew the promises we made in baptism when we rejected Satan and his works, and promised to serve God faithfully in his holy Catholic Church.

A fourteenth-century painting of the Resurrection.

Introduction to the renewal of baptismal vows at the Easter Vigil, The Sunday Missal.

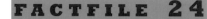

PILGRIMAGE

> The religious sense of the Christian people has always found expression in various forms of piety surrounding the Church's sacramental life, such as the veneration of relics, visits to sanctuaries, pilgrimages, etc.

Catechism of the Catholic Church (1674).

> In many circumstances, the Christian is called to make *promises* to God. Baptism and Confirmation, Matrimony and Holy Orders always entail promises. Out of personal devotion, the Christian may also promise to God this action, that prayer, this alms-giving, that pilgrimage, and so forth.

Catechism of the Catholic Church (2101).

A pilgrimage is a journey to a holy place for a religious reason. A pilgrimage may be one person or it may be a whole community travelling to perform a ritual together at a holy place. The important thing is that it is a journey to a religious place.

All religions have pilgrimage centres – Islam has Makkah, Hinduism has Benares on the River Ganges, Buddhism has Bodhgaya, Sikhism has Amritsar. Jerusalem is a major pilgrimage centre for Judaism, Islam and Christianity.

The other main Christian pilgrimage centres are Rome and Lourdes, but there are many other places of pilgrimage. In England alone there are centres such as Canterbury, Glastonbury, Lindisfarne and Walsingham.

A pilgrimage centre may be connected with a particularly holy person, e.g.:
- a place where a vision has been seen;
- a place where a relic (remains, such as a bone) of a saint is kept;
- a place connected with important events in the life of a holy person (St Thomas a Becket was murdered at Canterbury); or simply a place with a long history of pilgrimage.

Why people go on pilgrimage
- To feel some of the holiness of the place.
- To come closer to God.
- To seek God's forgiveness.
- To show devotion to God.
- To ask for and receive God's help (e.g. a cure for an illness).

The Shrine of Our Lady, Walsingham.

Jerusalem

Jerusalem is the main centre of pilgrimage for Christians, especially at Easter. The final week of Jesus' life on earth took place in Jerusalem. Pilgrims from all over the world flock to Jerusalem in the week before Easter to follow in the steps of Jesus. Many pilgrims try to re-enact events in Jesus' life by reading the Gospel stories at each place they visit.

On Good Friday they follow the *Via Dolorosa*, from the site of Pontius Pilate's headquarters to the site of the crucifixion, taking the route that Jesus did as he carried the cross. There are prayers and readings along the way. This pilgrim ritual is the basis of the Stations of the Cross.

The Church of the Holy Sepulchre contains the site of the crucifixion and the tomb of Jesus. The Roman Emperor Constantine built this church at his mother's (the Empress Helena) request after she made the first pilgrimage in 326.

"It was a magical experience which I can't really describe. I've been to lots of awesome places as a tourist, but travelling the Via Dolorosa was so different. I felt so close to Jesus, it felt like he was walking down that crowded street with me."

An English pilgrim to the Holy Land.

Pilgrims gather in St Peter's Square in Rome.

Rome

Rome is the pilgrimage centre for millions of Catholics. Catholics often visit Rome for the great festivals of Easter and Christmas for several reasons:

- There are seven pilgrim churches founded when the Roman Empire became Christian. Travelling the route to these churches has been a pilgrimage for over 1600 years.

- St Peter's Church was built by the Emperor Constantine over an earlier shrine which contained the tomb of St Peter, the leader of the twelve apostles of Jesus and the first Pope.

- The Church of St Paul outside the Walls was built by Constantine over the tomb of St Paul, the great Christian missionary, who wrote most of the epistles in the New Testament.

- Rome is the home of the Pope and the Vatican is the headquarters of the Catholic Church. A pilgrimage to Rome at the great festivals gives pilgrims the opportunity to go to Mass celebrated by the Pope and receive a papal blessing.

Lourdes

Lourdes is a much more recent pilgrimage site, but it is almost as popular as Rome and Jerusalem with over two million pilgrims a year.

Over a period of six months in 1858, the Blessed Virgin Mary appeared eighteen times to St Bernadette in a grotto just outside Lourdes in south west France. She revealed herself as the Immaculate Conception and caused a spring to flow in the grotto. Many pilgrims believe this spring has miraculous healing powers and over 5000 healing miracles are claimed to have occurred at Lourdes.

During the pilgrimage, there are special Masses, candlelight processions in the dark and many youth activities. Many young people come to Lourdes, often helping the sick who come for a cure. The special Lourdes hymn is sung during most of these activities. The highlight of the pilgrimage is to enter the grotto and bathe in the holy water.

Many sick pilgrims who have not been cured still claim that the pilgrimage has been really worthwhile because it has brought them closer to God and helped them to cope with their illness.

> Immaculate Mary our hearts are on fire.
> That title so wondrous fills all our desire.
> Ave, Ave, Ave Maria.

Lourdes hymn.

A procession at Lourdes.

QUESTIONS

Factfile 21 Advent and Christmas

1 Explain how Advent is a preparation for Christmas.

2 How and why do Christians celebrate Christmas?

Factfile 22 Lent and Holy Week

1 What event is Lent based on?

2 What are the main events of Holy Week?

3 Why is Holy Week important to Catholics?

4 "Good Friday is not good: it is the worst day in the history of the human race." Do you agree? Give reasons for your answer showing that you have considered another point of view.

Factfile 23 Easter and Pentecost

1 Make a list of the festivals of Easter.

2 Why do you think many Christians regard Easter as the most important festival?

3 "You should only celebrate festivals in church." Do you agree? Give reasons for your answer showing you have considered another point of view.

Factfile 24 Pilgrimage

1 Explain why Christians go on pilgrimage to Jerusalem.

2 "If God is everywhere, no places are especially holy, so pilgrimage is unnecessary." Do you agree? Give reasons for your answer showing you have considered another point of view.

7 MATTERS OF LIFE AND DEATH

CHRISTIAN TEACHINGS ON LIFE AFTER DEATH

There are two basic ideas about life after death:

RESURRECTION – AFTER DEATH NOTHING HAPPENS, UNTIL A TIME IN THE FUTURE (OFTEN CALLED THE LAST DAY OR THE DAY OF JUDGEMENT) WHEN THE DEAD WILL BE BROUGHT BACK TO LIFE (RAISED) AND BE GIVEN AN IMMORTAL (ETERNAL) BODY.

IMMORTALITY OF THE SOUL – THE BELIEF THAT HUMANS HAVE A BODY AND A SOUL (PERSONALITY, SELF) WHICH SURVIVES DEATH AND AFTER DEATH ENTERS A SPIRITUAL (NON-PHYSICAL) STATE WHERE GOD IS.

Most Jews believed in resurrection, but some were also influenced by the Greek idea of the immortality of the soul. Christian teaching includes both of these ideas.

> I look for the resurrection of the dead and the life of the world to come.

Nicene Creed.

Christians believe that at the end of the world (the Last Day when Jesus will return to the earth) the dead will be raised and will join the living before God who will judge them on the basis of their Christian faith and how they have lived their lives. Christians whose sins have been forgiven go to heaven and Christians who have sinned and not repented will go to hell. Some Christians believe that non-Christians go to hell, but others believe they will be given a chance to become Christians.

> I believe in ... the resurrection of the body and the life everlasting.

Apostle's Creed.

Christians also believe that your soul lives on and may go straight to heaven. Some do not believe in hell and think that there may be levels of heaven where people can continue their religious learning. Christians think that there will be an afterlife for all people and all religions, but how you have lived in this life affects what happens there.

> ... Christ has been raised from the dead, as the first-fruits of all who have fallen asleep. As it was by one man that death came, so through one man has come the resurrection of the dead. Just as all die in Adam, so in Christ all will be brought to life ... Someone may ask, How are dead people raised, and what sort of body do they have when they come? How foolish! What you sow must die before it is given new life; and what you sow is not the body that is to be, but only a bare grain, of wheat I dare say, or some other kind; it is God who gives it the sort of body that he has chosen for it, and for each kind of seed, its own kind of body ... It is the same too with the resurrection of the dead: what is sown is perishable, but what is raised is imperishable; what is sown is contemptible but what is raised is glorious; what is sown is weak, but what is raised is powerful ...

1 Corinthians 15:20-22,35-38,42-44.

'Resurrection of Christ and the Three Avogadori' by Tintoretto.

Catholic teaching on life after death

The *Catechism of the Catholic Church* teaches that:

1 'When we die those who have died in God's grace and are perfectly purified go to heaven.'
2 'Those who have died in God's grace but were imperfectly purified (those who die with unforgiven venial or lesser sins) will go to purgatory and be purified of their sins.'
3 'Those who have refused to believe or who die without repenting of a mortal sin will go to hell.'
4 'Jesus will come back to earth, the dead will be raised and all these souls will be reunited with their bodies.'
5 'Then God will judge everyone.'
6 'A new heaven and a new earth will be made and the resurrected from heaven will live there forever, but the resurrected from hell will return there forever.'

Extracted from Catechism of the Catholic Church (1020-1050).

The *Catechism* teaches that not only Christians will be in heaven because, 'Those who, through no fault of their own, do not know the Gospel of Christ or His Church, but who nevertheless, seek God with a sincere heart ... may achieve eternal salvation.' *(847.)*

Catholic funerals

Catholics hope to prepare for death with the sacraments of Anointing of the Sick, Penance (Reconciliation/Confession – see factfile 16), and *viaticum*. Strengthened and cleansed from all sin by these sacraments, Catholics believe that they will avoid hell and even the purification of purgatory

Some Catholics keep a vigil with the dead body either at home or in the church on the night before the funeral. This is an ancient custom probably reflecting a belief that the soul must be protected until it leaves the body after the funeral.

If the body is at home, it is brought to the church where it is received by the priest. Then there is a funeral Mass with hymns and various readings about life after death, prayers for the soul of the dead person (including absolution by the priest), a short talk about the life of the departed, and the Eucharist.

Just as Jesus died and rose again, so will the Father bring with him those who have died in Jesus. Just as in Adam all men die, so in Christ all will be made alive, alleluia.

Entrance antiphon from the Funeral Mass for the Easter season and All Souls Day Mass, The Sunday Missal.

I am the resurrection and the life, says the Lord. If anyone believes in me, even though he dies, he will live. Anyone who lives and believes in me will not die.

Communion antiphon from the Funeral Mass in Easter season and All Souls Day Mass, The Sunday Missal.

The body is then taken to the grave (or crematorium) where more prayers are said, the coffin is censed and sprinkled with holy water and the committal prayer is said: 'We have entrusted our brother/sister ... to God's merciful keeping, and we now commit his/her body to the ground: earth to earth, ashes to ashes, dust to dust; in sure and certain hope of the resurrection to eternal life through our Lord Jesus, who died, was buried, and rose again for us. To him be glory for ever and ever.'

We pray for our brother/sister N., who has died in Christ. Raise him/her at the last day to share in the glory of the risen Christ.

Opening prayer of the Funeral Mass, The Sunday Missal.

FACTFILE 26

THE SANCTITY OF LIFE

Christian teachings

Christians believe life is a gift from God and therefore it is sacred. Regarding life as sacred means it is to be treated as holy and therefore valued and preserved.

The sacredness of human life is seen especially by Christians in the life and death of Jesus. They believe that God sanctified human life by becoming human, and that the way Jesus suffered without attempting to do anything to cut short his sufferings shows that life is not to be ended except when God decides.

Human life is sacred because from its beginning it involves the creative action of God and it remains forever in a special relationship with the Creator, who is its sole end. God alone is the Lord of life from its beginning until its end: no one can under any circumstances claim for himself the right directly to destroy an innocent human being.

Catechism of the Catholic Church (2258).

God said, "Let us make man in our own image, in the likeness of ourselves, and let them be masters of the fish of the sea, the birds of heaven, the cattle, all the wild animals and all the creatures that creep along the ground." God created man in the image of himself, in the image of God he created him; male and female he created them ... God saw all he had made, and indeed it was very good ...

Genesis 1:26, 27, 31.

... while we are alive, we are living for the Lord, and when we die, we die to the Lord: and so, alive or dead, we belong to the Lord.

Romans 14:8.

Contraception

In 1798, Thomas Malthus published his *Theory of Population*. He argued that human population was growing faster than the earth's food resources and therefore humanity would have to control the population rise or face extinction by starvation. This made people think about controlling population growth and condoms were developed during the nineteenth century. In the 1950s the contraceptive pill was developed for women and became the main form of contraception. With the spread of Aids in the 1980s, a campaign was launched to encourage people to use condoms when having sex.

All these factors have led to a rapid rise in the use of contraceptives in Britain and it is estimated that about 90% of married couples use some form of contraception.

Catholic teaching on contraception

The Catholic Church has always taught that using 'artificial methods' is opposed to God's will. The Church teaches that sex should only take place within marriage. God gave human beings sex for married couples to enjoy and in order for them to reproduce. So every sexual act must be open to the possibility of conception and new life.

In '*Casti Conubii*', published in 1930, Pope Pius IX condemned all forms of artificial contraception. In 1951 Pope Pius XII declared that Catholics could use the rhythm method of contraception (restricting sex to the infertile period of a woman's menstrual cycle) as this was a natural way and part of God's creation. In 1968 Pope Paul VI's encyclical '*Humanae Vitae*' affirmed the teaching of previous popes that the only form of contraception allowable is the rhythm method. This teaching also appears in letters and encyclicals of Pope John Paul II and the *Catechism of the Catholic Church*.

Today, the Catholic Church regards contraception as a major cause of sexual promiscuity, broken families, the rise in divorce and sexually transmitted diseases, especially Aids. It claims that if sex is restricted to marriage without artificial contraception, then diseases will be reduced and the family restored.

Some Catholics, however, disagree with this teaching. Many use a letter published by the bishops of the United States, *Human Life in Our Day*, to justify using contraceptives. In this letter, the bishops recognised 'the pressures and circumstances which might reduce the moral guilt of those who use contraception.'

Attitudes of other Christians

Almost all non-Catholic Christians believe that contraception is permissible for Christians.

In 1930 the Lambeth Conference of the worldwide Anglican Communion (Church of England) declared that it was legitimate for Christians to use contraception to limit family size. This has been followed by the major Protestant Churches and the Orthodox Churches.

CONTRACEPTION AND ABORTION

> Called to give life, spouses share in the creative power and fatherhood of God. Married couples should regard it as their proper mission to transmit human life ...

Catechism of the Catholic Church (2367).

> For just reasons, spouses may wish to space the births of their children. It is their duty to make certain that their desire is not motivated by selfishness, but is in conformity with the generosity appropriate to responsible parenthood ... Methods of birth regulation based on self-observation and the use of infertile periods, is in conformity with the objective criteria of morality ... Every action which ... proposes, whether as an end or as a means, to render procreation impossible is intrinsically evil ...

Catechism of the Catholic Church (2368, 2370).

They believe contraception is right because it improves women's health and raises the standard of living and education for children because there are fewer of them.

They also believe that God created sex for enjoyment and to cement the bond of marriage; contraception within the confines of marriage allows this purpose of sex to be separated from the making of children.

> Some Christians object to any form of of contraception other than natural ... They hold it to be contrary to the natural law and the purpose of marriage to separate the unitive and procreative aspects of genital intercourse. The Methodist Church does not share these objections. It believes that responsible contraception is a welcome means towards fulfilment in marriage, the spacing of children, and the need, in some circumstances, to avoid pregnancy altogether for medical reasons. With the use of contraception, the unitive and creative aspects of intercourse can play their full part in the healing and development of a marriage.

Statement by the Methodist Church in 'What the Churches Say'.

Abortion

ABORTION – THE TERMINATION OF THE LIFE OF A FOETUS.

INFANTICIDE – KILLING A BABY AFTER BIRTH.

NATURAL ABORTION (MISCARRIAGE) – A FOETUS IS EXPELLED FROM THE UTERUS SPONTANEOUSLY (WITHOUT ANY ASSISTANCE).

PROCURED ABORTION – THE TERMINATION OF THE FOETUS WITH OUTSIDE HELP.

(IN THE REST OF THIS CHAPTER ABORTION WILL BE USED IN THE SENSE OF PROCURED ABORTION.)

ABORTION ON DEMAND – WOMEN BEING ALLOWED AN ABORTION WITHOUT ANY QUESTIONS ASKED.

Until 1967 all abortions in Great Britain were illegal which led to 'back street abortions' (women paying an unqualified person to give them an abortion). These often resulted in injury to the mother and sometimes death. The 1967 Abortion Act (amended in 1990) made abortions legal.

The 1990 Act states that abortions cannot take place after 24 weeks of pregnancy unless the mother's life is at risk because advances in medical techniques mean that such foetuses have a chance of survival.

The 1967 Act states that an abortion can be carried out if two doctors agree that:
- the mother's life is at risk;
- there is a risk of injury to the mother's physical or mental health;
- there is a risk that another child would put at risk the mental or physical health of existing children;
- there is a substantial risk that the baby might be born seriously handicapped.

Table of abortions carried out in England and Wales

1971	1991	1993
104,000	190,000	180,000
22% on women more than 12 weeks pregnant		12% on women more than 12 weeks pregnant

Source: Social Trends 25.

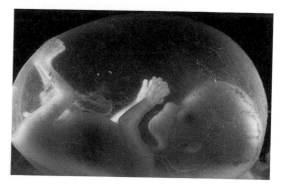

The human foetus after 14 weeks, surrounded by the fluid-filled amniotic sac. The foetus is recognisable as the infant it will become, though the head is still out-of-proportion.

The crucial issue for much discussion of abortion is, 'When does life begin?'

- **One view is that life begins at conception.**
  Many religions and anti-abortion groups such as Life believe that life begins as soon as the male sperm and female ovum combine.

- **Another view is that life begins at some definite point during pregnancy.**
  With the limited knowledge of biology at the time, some medieval philosophers argued that a foetus becomes a human being when the soul is implanted. They claimed that this happens to boys 40 days after conception and to girls 90 days after conception.

  Some used to consider that life began once the baby started moving in the womb. This was called the 'quickening'. Others consider that the baby should be considered an individual human being once it is capable of living outside the womb – once it becomes 'viable'.

- **A third view is that human life does not begin until birth:**

> I do not believe that a fertilised ovum is human life in the common sense meaning of the term. I believe human life begins at birth. Or, more technically, when a foetus is sufficiently developed to be capable of living if removed from the mother's womb.

Dee Wells quoted in 'Causing Death and Saving Lives', Julian Glover.

Another problem is whether there is a difference between contraception and abortion. Many arguments against abortion are based on the claim that if an abortion takes place, a human being who would have existed, now does not. If my mother had opted for an abortion, I would not be here now. But equally if my mother had used a more efficient method of contraception, I would not be here now. Is there really a difference between abortion and contraception?

The **doctrine of double effect** is often used in discussing both abortion and euthanasia. This is the idea that if I take an action to achieve one effect knowing that it will produce another, I cannot be blamed for the second effect. For example, if I remove a cancerous tumour from the womb of a pregnant woman, I know this will kill the foetus, but this is not an abortion, because my intention is simply to remove the cancer.

Jeremiah 1:5.

Is all this pain worth it?

Last year I became pregnant (I already have a three-year-old daughter). I was quite happy about it, but my partner went mad. He said it was the wrong time to have a child and we couldn't cope. He made me have an abortion which now I bitterly regret. I'm angry with myself because I wasn't strong enough to say no, and I'm very depressed. I resent my partner and I don't want anything to do with sex. Is this relationship worth the pain? Are my feelings normal? Will they ever change? Nobody knows about it, so I can't talk to anyone.

We affirm that every human life, created in the divine image, is unique ... and that this holds for each of us, born or yet to be born. We therefore believe that abortion is an evil ... and that abortion on demand would be a very great evil. But we also believe that to withdraw compassion is evil, and in circumstances of extreme distress or need, a very great evil ... Christians need to face frankly the fact that in an imperfect world the 'right' choice is sometimes the lesser of two evils.

Statement by the General Synod of the Church of England 1988 in 'What the Churches Say on Moral Issues'.

Catholics and abortion

The Catholic Church teaches that life begins at conception, so abortion is always wrong. It states that the natural law is that human life begins when an ovum is fertilised as there is an unbroken continuum from conception to birth. It is wrong to take life, therefore abortion is wrong.

It claims that every person has a natural 'right to life'. A foetus is a person and abortion destroys its right to life, so it follows that abortion is wrong.

Abortion can never be allowed for Catholics. The only possible exceptions are ectopic pregnancy or if the mother develops cancer. Either of these may kill the mother if untreated, but kill the foetus if treated. To deal with this problem, Catholics use the **doctrine of double effect** to say that the aim of removing the fallopian tube in an ectopic pregnancy is to save the mother's life, not kill the foetus. Therefore, as the death of the foetus is a second (double) effect which is not intended, the operation is permissible. Similarly, chemotherapy is not given to kill the foetus, but to kill the cancer, so the death of the foetus is a secondary, unintended effect. No abortion has been procured.

Human life must be respected and protected absolutely from the moment of conception. From the first moment of his existence, a human being must be recognised as having the rights of a person – among which is the inviolable right of every innocent being to life ... Abortion and infanticide are abominable crimes ... The law must provide appropriate penal sanctions for every deliberate violation of the child's rights.

Catechism of the Catholic Church (2270-71, 2273).

Other Christian attitudes to abortion

Non-Catholic Christians have two differing attitudes to abortion:

1 Some Conservative or fundamentalist Protestants have exactly the same view as Catholics. They believe that all abortion is wrong because life begins at the moment of conception and is totally sacred to God and all foetuses have a right to life.

2 Other Christians believe that abortion must be permitted in certain circumstances as the lesser of two evils, and so abortion is discouraged but not banned.

The unborn child is created in the image of God and is one for whom the Son of God died. This child is God's child. This child is part of God's world. So the life of this child is not ours to take. Therefore it is sin to take this child's life for reasons whether of birth control, gender selection, convenience, or avoidance of embarrassment.

From the Durham declaration to the United Methodist Church of the USA published in 'The Church and Abortion'.

EUTHANASIA – THE ACTION OF INDUCING A QUIET AND EASY DEATH.

There are several ways in which this can be done:

SUICIDE – A PERSON KNOWS THEY HAVE A PAINFUL, TERMINAL (WILL END IN DEATH) DISEASE AND COMMIT SUICIDE TO GIVE THEMSELVES A QUIET AND EASY DEATH.

ASSISTED SUICIDE – WHERE A PERSON HAS SUCH A PAINFUL TERMINAL DISEASE THAT THEY CANNOT OBTAIN THE MEANS FOR SUICIDE, SO THEY ASK SOMEONE TO GIVE THEM THE MEANS TO COMMIT SUICIDE.

VOLUNTARY EUTHANASIA – A PERSON WITH A PAINFUL, TERMINAL DISEASE WHO, UNABLE TO DO ANYTHING FOR THEMSELVES, ASKS SOMEONE ELSE TO KILL THEM PAINLESSLY, E.G. THE DOCTOR GIVES THEM A LETHAL DOSE OF PAINKILLERS.

NON-VOLUNTARY EUTHANASIA – A PERSON IS NOT KEPT ALIVE BECAUSE THEY ARE REGARDED AS HAVING A LIFE WORSE THAN DEATH, BUT CANNOT MAKE ANY DECISIONS FOR THEMSELVES, E.G. BABIES BORN WITH TERRIBLE ABNORMALITIES AND IN GREAT PAIN; PEOPLE ON LIFE-SUPPORT MACHINES WHO ARE 'BRAIN DEAD'; PEOPLE IN COMAS WHO HAVE TO BE FED INTRAVENOUSLY.

NOT STRIVING TO KEEP ALIVE

THE IDEA USED IN MEDICINE THAT IF SOMEONE IS SUFFERING FROM A TERMINAL ILLNESS, EVERYTHING POSSIBLE SHOULD BE DONE TO CURE THEM, AFTER THIS THEY SHOULD BE GIVEN PAINKILLERS. BUT IF, FOR EXAMPLE, THEY HAVE A HEART ATTACK, YOU DO NOT NEED TO GO THROUGH ALL THE RESUSCITATION PROCEDURES. THIS IS A VERY 'GREY' AREA IN BRITISH LAW AND MANY DOCTORS ARGUE THAT THEY HAVE TO STRIVE TO KEEP PEOPLE ALIVE OR THEY ARE ACTUALLY KILLING THEM.

LIVING WILL – WHEN SOMEONE MAKES A WILL WHICH STATES THAT IF THEY BECOME TERMINALLY ILL AND INCAPABLE OF MAKING DECISIONS FOR THEMSELVES, THEY WANT TO BE GIVEN A PAINLESS DEATH TO RELIEVE THEM OF THEIR SUFFERING. THESE WILLS ARE RECOMMENDED BY THE VOLUNTARY EUTHANASIA SOCIETY FOR THOSE WHO DO NOT WANT TO LIVE FOR YEARS IN PAIN, DISTRESS, OR ON A LIFE-SUPPORT MACHINE.

DOUBLE EFFECT – THIS SAME IDEA IS USED IN ABORTION. IT IS ALL RIGHT TO GIVE A PATIENT DRUGS TO RELIEVE THEIR PAIN, KNOWING THAT THEY WILL KILL THEM OVER A PERIOD OF TIME, BECAUSE YOUR AIM IS TO RELIEVE THE PAIN, NOT KILL THEM. IT IS USUALLY CLAIMED THAT THIS IS VERY DIFFERENT FROM GIVING THEM ONE DOSE OF PAINKILLERS SUFFICIENT TO KILL THEM STRAIGHT AWAY.

FACTFILE 28

EUTHANASIA

Thou shalt not kill, but needs't not strive Officiously to keep alive.

'The Latest Decalogue',
A.H. Clough.

> **Naked I came from my mother's womb, naked I shall return again. Yahweh gave, Yahweh has taken back. Blessed be the name of Yahweh!**

Job 1:21.

> Whatever its motives and means, direct euthanasia consists in putting an end to the lives of handicapped, sick, or dying persons. It is morally unacceptable. Thus an act or omission which, of itself or by intention, causes death in order to eliminate suffering constitutes a murder greatly contrary to the dignity of the human person and to the respect due to the living God, his Creator.

Catechism of the Catholic Church (2277).

Catholics and euthanasia

The Catholic Church teaches that all forms of euthanasia are wrong.

1   Catholics regard suicide as wrong because of their view on the sanctity of life. Life is created by God and so it is sacred to God. It is up to God, not us, when we die. To commit suicide, therefore, is to put yourself on a par with God which is condemned in the Scriptures.

2   Catholics regard assisted suicide, voluntary euthanasia and non-voluntary suicides as wrong because they are a form of murder. People are taking upon themselves God's role which is a grave sin. It is up to God to decide when to take a person's life, and humans should not interfere with that process.

> Even if death is thought imminent, the ordinary care owed to a sick person cannot be legitimately interrupted.

Catechism of the Catholic Church (2279).

3   Not striving to keep alive causes problems for religious believers. The Catholic Church accepts that treatments which prolong life, but do not cure, do not need to be given if the patient does not want them. Drastic chemotherapy, for example, causes pain and discomfort to a cancer patient but may only give them a few more weeks of life.

However, this should only be in exceptional cases, because by stopping all drugs it could be direct euthanasia.

> Discontinuing medical procedures that are burdensome, dangerous, extraordinary, or disproportionate to the expected outcome can be legitimate; it is the refusal of 'over-zealous' treatment.

Catechism of the Catholic Church (2278).

4   For Catholics, the doctrine of double effect means that terminally ill patients can be given increasing doses of painkillers, even though it will shorten their lives, but not a large enough dose to end life immediately.

> The use of painkillers to alleviate the suffering of the dying, even at the risk of shortening their days, can be morally in conformity with human dignity if death is not willed either as an end or a means, but only foreseen and tolerated as inevitable.

Catechism of the Catholic Church (2279).

5   Many Catholics regard switching off a life-support machine as direct euthanasia. They certainly do not allow switching off a life-support machine and then allowing the patient to starve to death.

Other Christian attitudes to euthanasia

Most non-Catholic Christians have exactly the same views about euthanasia as Catholics with two exceptions:

- some would allow the switching off of life-support machines and the removal of artificial feeding;
- some would regard suicide as acceptable because they believe if people are in so much pain that they do not know how else to cope, God will not regard suicide as a sin.

> The common experience of Christians throughout the ages has been that the grace of God sustains heart and mind to the end. To many, the end of life is clouded by pain and impaired judgement, and whilst we believe that it is right to use all and any medical treatment to control pain, experience denies the rightness of legalising the termination of life by a doctor, authorised by a statement signed by the patient whilst in health. Such euthanasia threatens to debase the function of doctors and impairs the confidence of their patients.

Statement by the Salvation Army in 'What the Churches Say on Moral Issues'.

QUESTIONS

Factfile 25 Christian Teachings on life after death

1 Have a class discussion on whether there is life after death. Then write down the main arguments for and against.

2 Make a chart to show the main differences between resurrection of the body and immortality of the soul.

3 "Once you're dead, you're dead. There can be no life after death." Do you agree? Give reasons for your answer, showing that you have considered another point of view.

4 What Catholic beliefs about life after death are shown in a Catholic funeral?

Factfile 26 The Sanctity of Life

1 Write down three reasons why Christians believe life is sacred.

Factfile 27 Contraception and Abortion

1 Explain why Catholics are opposed to contraception.

2 Why do some other Christians allow contraception?

3 Have a class discussion on why abortion was legalised in Britain and whether the law now needs to be changed.

4 "No Catholic should ever have an abortion." Do you agree? Give reasons for your answer, showing that you have considered another point of view.

Factfile 28 Euthanasia

1 Write down the differences between suicide, voluntary euthanasia and involuntary euthanasia.

2 Discuss in a group why euthanasia has become more of an issue in the last twenty years.

3 Write down two Catholic arguments against euthanasia.

4 "If I were on a life-support machine and brain dead, I would want my relatives or friends to switch it off." Do you agree? Give your reasons, showing that you have considered another point of view.

LOVING ONE'S NEIGHBOUR – CHRISTIAN DISCIPLESHIP

Christian values are based on the ten commandments as given to Moses and the two commandments which Jesus gave to his disciples.

The **ten commandments** can be divided into:

Respect for God
- Worship God alone.
- Do not make images of God.
- Do not use God's name wrongly.
- Keep the Sabbath day holy.

Respect for other people
- Respect your parents.
- Do not murder.
- Do not commit adultery.
- Do not steal.
- Do not lie.
- Do not covet.

The **two commandments** also concern God and other people.
1 Love God with all your heart, mind and strength (this summarises the first four commandments).
2 Love your neighbour as yourself (this summarises the last six commandments).

The *Catechism of the Catholic Church* explains how these commandments should be revealed in the life of a Christian in Part Three, 'Life in Christ', Section 2.

'Moses receives the ten commandments' by Julius Schnorr von Carolsfeld.

FACTFILE 29

CHRISTIAN VALUES: THE SERMON ON THE MOUNT

The commandments, 'you shall not commit adultery, you shall not kill, you shall not steal, you shall not covet', and any other commandment, are summed up in this sentence, 'You shall love your neighbour as yourself.'

Catechism of the Catholic Church (2055).

I am the Lord your God, who brought you out of the land of Egypt, out of the place of slave-labour ... You will have no gods other than me ... You must not misuse the name of Yahweh ... Observe the Sabbath day and keep it holy ... Honour your father and mother ... You must not kill ... You must not commit adultery ... You must not steal ... You must not give false evidence against your fellow ... You must not set your heart on your neighbour's spouse, you must not set your heart on ... any of your neighbour's possessions.

The ten commandments, Deuteronomy 5:6-21.

The Sermon on the Mount

Jesus explained how to love your neighbour in the Sermon on the Mount (*Matthew* chapters 5,6,7). He said that a Christian should fulfil the Law of Moses in the following ways:

1 You shall not kill (5:21-26) is a command not to be angry with your brother and always to seek reconciliation.

2 You shall not commit adultery (5:27-30) is a command not to look with lust on someone who is married.

3 No divorce without a certificate (5:31-32) is a total ban on divorce.

4 No swearing falsely (5:33-37) is a total ban on using God's name in any dealings. Christians are to be so honest that they do not need to swear (make an oath as in courts where people swear on the Bible), they should just say 'Yes' or 'No'.

5 An eye for an eye (5:38-42) is developed into a ban on all forms of revenge. Moses allowed revenge but restricted it to what had been done (an eye for an eye, not a life for an eye), but Jesus said that his way is to seek reconciliation – turning the other cheek if hit, giving their shirt if asked for their coat, walking two miles if forced to walk one.

6 Displaying religion (6:1-18). Jesus said that his followers are not to show off about how religious they are (as some of the people at the time of Jesus did).
If Christians give to the poor, they should do it secretly or anonymously.
When Christians pray they must not do it out on the street, but in private.
Nor should they should make very long prayers, God does not need to be told things.
All Christians need is the **LORD'S PRAYER** because it has:
adoration – 'Our Father in heaven, may your name be held holy, your kingdom come, your will be done on earth as in heaven';
requests and thanksgiving – 'give us today our daily bread' is thanksgiving for God's gifts; 'forgive us our debts' is confession of our sins; 'as we have forgiven those who are in debt to us' is a desire for reconciliation; 'And do not put us to the test, but save us from the Evil One' are requests for help in Christian living.

> Our Father, who art in heaven,
> hallowed be thy name;
> Thy kingdom come;
> Thy will be done on earth as it is in heaven.
> Give us this day our daily bread;
> and forgive us our trespasses
> as we forgive those who trespass against us;
> and lead us not into temptation,
> but deliver us from evil.

The Lord's Prayer, The Sunday Missal.

No one should know when Christians fast. They should behave to the outside world as if they were not fasting. Fasting should be done for God, not to show off to other people.

7   Christians and Money (6:19-34). Jesus said that his followers are not to be concerned about money. They should try to live the sort of life that gives treasure in heaven not on earth. If they search for money they will start to be ruled by it when they should be ruled by God. Jesus said that God cares for people's physical needs just as he cares for the birds and flowers. Christians should get on with doing what God wants rather than worrying what is going to happen tomorrow or where their money is to come from.

8   Judgement (7:1-5). Jesus said that his followers do not judge other people. They look for what is wrong with themselves and put that right first.

9   The Golden Rule (7:7-12). Jesus said that God is ready to give his followers what they ask for. In the same way Christians are to always treat other people as they would want to be treated themselves.

10 The Narrow Way (7:13-14). Jesus told his followers that the path you have to follow to get to heaven is difficult and narrow whereas the road that leads to hell is wide and easy. But the narrow way is the only one to follow.

11 Signs of Discipleship (7:15-23). Jesus warned that there would be false prophets who would claim to be his followers. He said that the only way to decide whether a religious leader is a true follower of Jesus is by their actions. Just as a farmer judges a tree by its fruit and cuts down what does not produce good fruit, so God judges by people's actions. Jesus said that calling him 'Lord' or even casting out devils in his name is not enough. What matters is to do what God has told us to do (follow the teachings of Jesus).

12 The houses on sand and rock (7:24-27). As a final illustration of discipleship, Jesus told a parable to show that it is necessary not just to listen to the words of Jesus, but also to put them into action. Someone who does this is like a person who builds his house on rock foundations which can stand against any storm. Someone who listens but does not put it into practice is like a person who builds his house on sand. At the first sign of bad weather his house will collapse. Christians who follow the commandments and the teachings in the Sermon on the Mount will have a secure life.

OTHER NEW TESTAMENT TEACHING ON CHRISTIAN VALUES

Jesus' invitation to enter his kingdom comes in the form of *parables*, a characteristic feature of his teaching. Through his parables he invites people to the feast of his kingdom, but he also asks for a radical choice: to gain the kingdom, one must give everything. Words are not enough; deeds are required. The parables are like mirrors for man: will he be hard soil or good earth for the word? What use has he made of the talents he has received? Jesus and the presence of the kingdom in this world are secretly at the heart of the parables. One must enter the kingdom, that is, become a disciple of Christ, in order to 'know the secrets of the kingdom of heaven'. For those who stay 'outside', everything remains enigmatic.

Catechism of the Catholic Church (546).

Features of discipleship

1 **The Commission** *(Matthew* 28:18-20). Before his ascension Jesus told his disciples to make disciples of all nations, to baptise people in the name of the Trinity, and to teach people to follow all of his commands.

2 **The Good Samaritan** *(Luke* 10:25-37). In this parable Jesus taught his disciples that loving your neighbour means helping anyone in trouble, even your worst enemy. The parable tells of a Jew being badly beaten by robbers. He was ignored by a priest and a Levite (a Temple official) who should have helped a fellow Jew, but walked by on the other side (perhaps in case they were attacked). However, a Samaritan (a bitter enemy, because Jews and Samaritans disagreed about how and where God should be worshipped), stopped and took him to an inn and paid for his accommodation there. So a feature of discipleship is to help anyone regardless of race or religion.

3 **Parables of the Kingdom** *(Matthew* 13). The parable of the sower shows that Christians must listen and act on God's word and God will bring a great harvest despite great difficulties.
The parable of the mustard seed shows that Christianity will have great results from small beginnings.
The parable of the leaven shows that a few Christian disciples will change many people, just as a small amount of yeast changes a large amount of bread dough.
The parable of the weeds and the net show that Christian disciples should get on with the job and not worry that evil people are working alongside them, because in the end, God sorts everything out and rewards good people and punishes evil people.
The parables of the hidden treasure and the pearl of great price show that it is worth giving up everything for the rewards of God's kingdom which will be given to disciples.

4 **Status of discipleship** *(Matthew* 20:24-28). Jesus said that the life of his followers is quite different from that of leaders of the world. In Christianity leaders are servants and ready to give up their lives as Jesus did.

Christian justice and reconciliation

1 The Parable of the Forgiving Father (*Luke* 15:11-32).
Jesus told a parable about a young son who is sick of being at home, and asks his father for his share of the inheritance. He ends up looking after the pigs and eating their food after blowing it all on high living in the city, so he returns home to get a job as a labourer. But his father, overjoyed to see him, forgives him and throws a party for his son.

Jesus told this parable to show his followers that they must forgive those who repent and be reconciled with them. It also shows that God's forgiveness is for everyone, and that Jews and Gentiles are equal before God (in looking after pigs, the younger son had become unclean, like a Gentile).

2 Respect for all people (*James* 2:1-9). The apostle James said that Christians must never treat any type or class of person better than another. In particular they must not show favour to the wealthy because God has shown favour to the poor who tend to be oppressed by the rich.

Loving your neighbour means respecting all people.

Christian responsibility

1 The Parable of the Talents (*Matthew* 25:14-30). In this parable Jesus taught that Christians must share their gifts and use them for God and for others. He tells a story of a ruler who gave each of his servants a talent (large amount of money) and went away to another country. When he came back he rewarded those servants who had used the money to make more money, but punished the servant who simply kept the money safe.

2 The Parable of the Sheep and the Goats (*Matthew* 25:31-46). Jesus told a story about the end of the world and how everyone will be judged and separated into the good and bad in the way that a shepherd separates sheep and goats. The good are those who have helped the hungry, thirsty, homeless, ill and prisoners. The bad are those who refused to help all these victims. To emphasise his teaching that Christians must help, Jesus said that in helping the starving, homeless etc., you are helping him; and in refusing to help them, you are refusing to help him.

3 Sickness and Healing (*James* 5:13-15). James says that if Christians are suffering, they should pray; and if they are sick, they should ask the elders of the Church to anoint them with oil and pray over them, and this will cure them.

Christians today both pray for the sick and help them practically. Some Christians think this also means that there should be healing services.

Caring for the sick is an important expression of Christian responsibility.

4 The Parable of the Unmerciful Servant (*Matthew* 18:23-35). Jesus told a story about a servant who owed his master a huge amount of money which he could not repay. He begged his master to give him extra time to pay and instead his master let him off the whole debt. The servant immediately went round to another servant who owed him a very small amount of money and demanded repayment. The man begged for more time, but the servant refused and had the poor man imprisoned for debt. The servant's master was furious when he found out, and ordered a massive punishment for the servant.

Jesus told this story to show Christians that just as they have received mercy from God they must show mercy and forgiveness to other people.

FACTFILE 31

THE EXPRESSION OF CHRISTIAN VALUES

Christians express their values in many ways:

1 By service to others

Christians often have jobs like teaching which is service to others. They also show service to others in their spare time by doing voluntary work in youth clubs, running lunch clubs for seniors, and working for charitable groups like Citizens of the Society of St Vincent de Paul (see factfile 55).

2 Through compassion for those who suffer

Christians are to be found in all the caring professions such as nursing, social work and working with the handicapped. Christians also started the hospice movement which seeks to help those with terminal diseases come to terms with death and die surrounded by love. Many Christians, inspired by their beliefs, spend their spare time working for the Red Cross, with the homeless and through soup runs.

3 In concern for the causes of suffering

Christians are concerned about the causes of suffering and some become involved in the work of CAFOD or in politics in order to remove the causes of suffering. In their statement *The Common Good,* published in 1996, the Catholic Bishops of England and Wales pointed to ways of removing the suffering of unemployment. Employers should not sack people just to increase the profits of the shareholders. In the same way, CAFOD asks Catholics to provide money for wells to remove the suffering caused by lack of clean water.

4 By helping those in need

Christian values such as those expressed in the parable of the sheep and the goats compel Christians to help those in need. The Catholic Church has groups in every diocese to help the poor and homeless. It supports the work of CAFOD in helping the poor and starving in developing countries.

5 In seeking justice for the oppressed

Christians work for justice all over the world. The Catholic Church in South and Central America works for justice for the homeless and jobless. In South Africa it worked for justice for black Africans by opposing apartheid.

Mother Teresa

Mother Teresa is one of the most famous exemplary Christians of the twentieth century. See factfile 48 for information on her life and work.

Helder Camara

Helder Camara was born in Brazil in 1909. He entered a seminary in 1923 and was ordained in 1931. During his early years as a priest, he thought that the Church should support all governments. In 1952, he became bishop of Rio de Janeiro and started to visit the shanty towns that were developing on the edges of the city. As he read the teachings of Jesus about money and concern for the poor, he began to see that it was sinful that a city like Rio had fantastic wealth in places like the Copacabana, but terrible poverty in the shanty towns.

Camara was Archbishop of Recife (1964-1984), in a very poor area of North East Brazil largely ignored by the government. He continued to work with the poor and began to challenge the government to do something about the state of the poor. Camara supported the many priests in his dioceses who were involved in the development of **Liberation Theology**. This theology looks at the life and teaching of Jesus from the viewpoint of the poor. It sees the Sermon on the Mount and such parables as the sheep and the goats as a call for the Church to stand alongside the poor and try to force the authorities to do something about poverty. It claims that Jesus came to liberate the poor from poverty as well as sin.

Camara was attacked by the Brazilian government which saw him as a dangerous revolutionary. He was also attacked by priests like Camillo Torres who thought priests should join guerilla fighters. Camara was influenced by Martin Luther King and refused to have anything to do with violence. He believed that Christians must follow the example of Jesus and renounce all forms of violence. But at the same time, he believed that Christians should challenge governments which allow the rich to live off the labour of the poor.

Helder Camara was nominated for the Nobel Peace Prize in the late seventies. This was opposed by the Brazilian and American governments because of his revolutionary statements.

> **The Spirit of the Lord is on me, for he has anointed me to bring good news to the afflicted. He has sent me to proclaim liberty to captives, sight to the blind, to let the oppressed go free, to proclaim a year of favour from the Lord.**

Luke 4:18-19, a quotation from Isaiah 61:1-2 used by Jesus in his preaching at the synagogue in Nazareth: an inspiration for Helder Camara.

TWO EXEMPLARY CHRISTIANS OF THE TWENTIETH CENTURY

Dom Helder Camara.

QUESTIONS

Factfile 29 Christian Values: The Sermon on the Mount

1 Explain how the two commandments of Jesus summarises the Ten Commandments.

2 Why do you think Catholics replaced the Sabbath with Sunday?

3 Give three teachings from the Sermon on the Mount about how to treat other people.

4 What does the Sermon on the Mount teach about prayer?

Factfile 30 Other New Testament Teaching on Christian Values

1 Name three parables Jesus told about discipleship.

2 What is the meaning of the parable of the forgiving father?

3 What does the parable of the sheep and the goats teach about Christian responsibility?

Factfile 31 The Expression of Christian Values

1 List five ways in which Christians show their values.

2 "It doesn't matter what you believe as long as you love your neighbour." Do you agree? Give reasons for your answer, showing you have considered another point of view.

Factfile 32 Exemplary Christians of the Twentieth Century

1 Make a list of the things Mother Teresa has done in her life (use factfile 48).

2 Why do you think Helder Camara was opposed by the Brazilian government ?

MARRIAGE AND FAMILY LIFE

MARRIAGE – 'CONDITION OF MAN AND WOMAN LEGALLY UNITED FOR PURPOSE OF LIVING TOGETHER AND, USUALLY, CREATING LAWFUL OFFSPRING.'

COHABITATION – 'LIVING TOGETHER AS HUSBAND AND WIFE WHEN NOT MARRIED TO EACH OTHER.'

PROMISCUITY – 'HAVING SEXUAL RELATIONS NOT LIMITED BY MARRIAGE OR COHABITATION, CASUAL SEX.'

ADULTERY – 'VOLUNTARY SEXUAL INTERCOURSE OF MARRIED PERSON OTHER THAN WITH SPOUSE.'

MONOGAMY – MARRIAGE TO ONLY ONE PARTNER.

POLYGAMY – MARRIAGE TO MORE THAN ONE PARTNER AT THE SAME TIME.

SERIAL MONOGAMY – MARRIAGE TO SEVERAL PEOPLE IN YOUR LIFETIME, BUT SEPARATED BY DIVORCE SO THAT YOU ARE ONLY MARRIED TO ONE PARTNER AT A TIME.

Factfile 33

SOCIAL FACTS ON MARRIAGE, DIVORCE AND FAMILY LIFE

TABLE 1 Marriage 1971-1993 England and Wales

	1971	1989	1993
Number of marriages (thousands)	405	347	299
First marriage	79%	63%	61%
mean age for men (years)	24.6	26.9	28.0
mean age for women (years)	22.6	24.8	26.0
Teenage marriages			
Brides	27%	8%	–
Grooms	9%	2%	–
Cohabitation before marriage	7%	48%	–
Likelihood of being married before the age of 50			
Men	95%	77%	–
Women	93%	78%	–

Source: Social Trends 25.

Half of marriages take place in a church. Many people marry without a religious ceremony as half the number of marriages take place in registry offices. These are known as civil marriages and require the couple undertake to stay with each other for life. Since 1995 civil marriages do not have to take place in a registry office; people can now marry anywhere provided that the place is registered.

DIVORCE – 'THE LEGAL TERMINATION OF A MARRIAGE SO THAT THE SPOUSES ARE FREE TO MARRY SOMEONE ELSE.'

In the British legal system, a person must be divorced before they remarry, otherwise they commit bigamy which is a criminal offence.

TABLE 2 Changes in the divorce law of the UK

	YEAR
Divorce only allowed by Act of Parliament	1534
Civil divorce allowed on grounds of adultery only	1857
Desertion, cruelty and insanity allowed as grounds	1937
Irretrievable breakdown and cheaper divorce introduced	1969

Problem pages are full of letters about the problems of relationships, adultery and divorce.

My parents are getting divorced

My parents are in their 50s and divorcing (20 years too late, I think). I love them both, but they want me to take sides. Where do I turn?

I want him back

My boyfriend told me he doesn't want to be with me and my son any more. We've been seeing each other for four years, he's 26 and I'm 32 with a six-year old son from a previous relationship. He didn't want to get married to settle down so we didn't live together and both of us continued to see our own friends. I was happy with this and I desperately want him back.

He won't leave his wife

I had an affair with a man at work a few years ago, but we went our separate ways when his wife became pregnant. I soon married and had children, but luck or fate intervened and we are together again.

I've left my husband and children and prepared a home for us to move into. I know he loves me and he says that he doesn't love his wife, but he won't leave his children.

How can I make him see sense and make the break? I can offer him a better life and when his children see how happy their dad is, they would accept the situation.

TABLE 3 Divorce 1961-1993 England and Wales

	1961	1971	1981	1991	1993
Number of divorces (thousands)	25	74	146	151	165
Divorce rate (divorces per 1000 population)	2.1	5.9	11.9	12.7	–
Children (aged under 16) of divorcing couples (thousands)	35*	82	159	148	176
Lone parents (thousands)	–	570	–	1010	–

* = all children no statistics for under 16's

Source: Social Trends 25.

Statements on divorce from a newspaper in 1995.

The charity One plus One last month published a report claiming to show that married people live longer, have healthier lives, suffer less stress and mental illness and are financially better off than the single, divorced or widowed. Fiona McAllister, the researcher who wrote the charity's report, drew on evidence from across Europe and the United States to demonstrate the link between marital breakdown and physical and mental ill-health... Data from the Office of Population Censuses and Surveys, she claimed, showed that divorced men aged 45-49 had a 76% extra risk of premature death compared with those in marriages. For women of the same age, she found a 39% extra risk.

Ms McAllister concedes that it may be that better balanced and healthier people are more likely to marry and stay wed, but believes the main reason for marriage's protective effect is that the institution provides support against stress and anxiety.

Denise Knowles of Relate, the national relationship counselling agency, said yesterday 'divorce probably should carry a health warning... However we do believe that there has to be a case for divorce when people find themselves locked in a physically or mentally violent relationship where fear and intimidation are part of daily existence. That is not a healthy relationship for adults, or children.'

Doctor Patrick Dixon author of a recent book, *The Rising Price of Love*, said divorce would also have long-term effects on children in the families concerned, 'Divorce often means poor exam results, damaged health and stress, four times the risk of needing psychiatric help as a child and a greater risk of breakdown in middle age.'

TABLE 4 BIRTHS OUTSIDE MARRIAGE

	1971	1977	1981	1989	1993
Percentage of births	8	10	13	27	32
Percentage of joint registrations (likely to indicate parents living together)	46	–	–	71	75

Source: Social Trends 25.

Family types

NUCLEAR FAMILY – TWO PARENTS AND THEIR CHILDREN LIVING TOGETHER ALONE.

EXTENDED FAMILY – GRANDPARENTS, PARENTS, AUNTS, UNCLES, COUSINS AND CHILDREN; EITHER LIVING TOGETHER OR LIVING CLOSE ENOUGH TO SEE EACH OTHER REGULARLY.

ONE PARENT FAMILY – ONE PARENT LIVING WITH CHILDREN ALONE; THIS CAN BE BECAUSE OF DIVORCE, SEPARATION, DEATH OF MARRIAGE PARTNER OR BEING AN UNMARRIED PARENT.

IN THE 1991 CENSUS ONLY 16% OF ASIAN FAMILIES IN THE UK WERE LIVING AS EXTENDED FAMILIES.

The most important thing in life is to love your children as much as you possibly can.

Can Patsy Palmer (Bianca in 'Eastenders') keep to her claim when she is a single mother?

TABLE 5 FAMILIES WITH DEPENDENT CHILDREN

Family Type	1971	1975	1981	1989
2 parent	92%	90%	87%	81%
Single mother	1%	1%	2%	6%
Divorced/separated mother	4%	5%	6%	11%
Widowed mother	2%	2%	2%	1%
Lone father	1%	1%	2%	2%

Christian attitudes to sex

The Catholic Church teaches that sex belongs exclusively to a man and woman married to each other. Catholics believe that sex was given to us by God for the procreation of children so it must take place within marriage. Therefore, premarital sex and cohabitation are wrong. Adultery is also wrong – it is condemned in the Ten Commandments and by Jesus in the Gospels.

Most non-Catholic Christians also believe that premarital sex, cohabitation and adultery are sinful.

Some Christians accept that couples may live together before marriage, but they would expect them to marry when starting a family and would only accept a sexual relationship between two people committed to a long-term relationship. A report published by the Church of England's Board of Responsibility in 1995, *Something to Celebrate,* said that cohabiting couples should be welcomed and supported by the Church, 'recognising that for many this is a step along the way to the fuller commitment of marriage'. There have been similar reports by the Methodist Church and the Society of Friends (Quakers).

> The sexual act must take place exclusively within marriage. Outside marriage it always constitutes a grave sin and excludes one from sacramental communion.
> Some today claim a 'right to a trial marriage' where there is an intention of getting married later. However firm the purpose of those who engage in premature sexual relations may be, 'the fact is that such liaisons can scarcely ensure mutual sincerity and fidelity in a relationship between a man and a woman' ... Human love does not tolerate 'trial marriages'. It demands a total and definitive gift of persons to one another.

Catechism of the Catholic Church (2390-91).

FACTFILE 34

CHRISTIAN TEACHINGS ON MARRIAGE AND DIVORCE

Among you there must be not even a mention of sexual vice or impurity in any of its forms ...

Ephesians 5:3.

Carey speaks out on 'living in sin'

"A provisional, purely private arrangment is not as good a framework as marriage for the nurture of families."

Hugh Grant and Liz Hurley. Many people choose to live together without getting married.

> The matrimonial covenant, by which a man and a woman establish between themselves a partnership of the whole of life, is by its nature ordered toward the good of the spouses and the procreation and education of offspring; this covenant between baptised persons has been raised by Christ the Lord to the dignity of a sacrament.

Catechism of the Catholic Church (1601).

Catholic teaching on marriage

The Catholic Church teaches that God created man and woman for each other.

Marriage has three purposes: the good of the couple (it enables them to have a life-long relationship of love) and the procreation of children and their education. These purposes are outlined in the wedding service:

> N and N (Christian names only) you have come together in this Church so that the Lord may seal and strengthen your love in the presence of the Church's minister and this community. Christ abundantly blesses this love. He has already consecrated you in baptism and now he enriches and strengthens you by a special sacrament so that you may assume the duties of marriage in mutual and lasting fidelity. And so, in the presence of the Church, I ask you to state your intentions ... Are you ready freely and without reservation to give yourselves to each other in marriage? Are you ready to love and honour each other as man and wife for the rest of your lives? Are you ready to accept children lovingly from God, and bring them up according to the law of Christ and his Church?

Roman Catholic Rite of Marriage During Mass.

The other main features of a Catholic marriage service are:

1 readings from the Bible and a short talk on the nature of Christian marriage;
2 exchange of vows committing the partners to lifetime marriage;
3 exchange of rings symbolising the unending nature of marriage;
4 prayers asking God's blessing on the couple and the help of the Holy Spirit to make the marriage work;
5 communion uniting the couple with Christ and each other.

> From a valid marriage arises a *bond* between the spouses which by its very nature is perpetual and exclusive; furthermore, in a Christian marriage the spouses are strengthened and, as it were, consecrated for the duties and the dignity of their state *by a special sacrament.*

Catechism of the Catholic Church (1638).

> Lord, in your love you have given us this Eucharist to unite us with one another and with you. As you have made N and N one in this sacrament of marriage and in the sharing of the one bread and the one cup, so now make them one in love for one another.

Prayer after communion from the Wedding Mass.

Catholic teaching on divorce

The Catholic Church does not allow divorce because:

a) Jesus taught that divorce is wrong – 'Back in the house, the disciples questioned him again about this, and he said to them, "Whoever divorces his wife and marries another is guilty of adultery against her. And if a woman divorces her husband and marries another, she is guilty of adultery too."' *(Mark 10:10-12.)*

b) The couple have made a covenant with God in the sacrament of marriage and that covenant cannot be broken by any earthly power – 'Thus the *marriage bond* has been established by God himself in such a way that a marriage concluded and consummated between baptised persons can never be dissolved.' *(Catechism of the Catholic Church 1640.)*

However, the Catholic Church does allow **annulment** (a declaration that the marriage was never a true marriage and so the partners are free to marry) if:

a) one partner was forced into the marriage;

b) one partner suffered from mental problems at the time of the marriage;

c) one partner did not intend to keep the marriage vows;

d) one of the partners was not baptised at the time of the marriage.

Each diocese has a Marriage Tribunal to decide on applications for annulment because there are too many for the Pope alone to consider.

This couple have remarried although they have both been divorced.

Most non-Catholic Churches allow divorced people to remarry, but they usually require them to talk to the minister about why their first marriages failed. They are sometimes asked to show repentance for the failure and required to promise that this time their marriage will be for life. Many Christians do not approve of divorce. They believe that you cannot take life-long vows twice and that Jesus banned divorce. Others claim that Jesus allowed divorce in *Matthew* 19:9, and that as Christians are allowed forgiveness and a new chance for confessed sins, so they should have another chance at marriage as long as they are determined to make it work this time.

> The remarriage of persons divorced from a living, lawful spouse contravenes the plan and law of God as taught by Christ. They are not separated from the Church, but they cannot receive Eucharistic communion. They will lead Christian lives especially by educating their children in the faith.

Catechism of the Catholic Church (1665).

FACTFILE 35

CATHOLIC TEACHING ON THE FAMILY

> Lord by this sacrament you make us one family in Christ your Son, one in the sharing of his body and blood, one in the communion of his Spirit. Help us grow in love for one another and come to the full maturity of the Body of Christ.

Prayer from Roman Catholic Baptismal Mass, The Sunday Missal.

> Children be obedient to your parents in the Lord, – that is what uprightness demands. The first commandment that has a promise attached to it is: 'Honour your father and your mother' and the promise is: 'so that you may have long life and prosper in the land.' And parents, never drive your children to resentment but bring them up with correction and advice inspired by the Lord.

Ephesians 6:1-4.

One of the main purposes of marriage is to have children and bring them up in a secure and loving Christian environment so that they will come to love God and follow Jesus. The teaching on divorce makes it clear that Christian parents should stay together and bring up their children together.

The *Catechism* emphasises that the family is the basic unit of society. The *Book of Genesis* describes how God instituted the family. After creating male and female God told them to 'be fruitful and multiply' (*Genesis* 1:27-28). *Genesis* 2:24 describes how marriage was instituted as the way to bring up children. This is emphasised further in the New Testament in *Ephesians* 5:22-6:4 where Paul writes about Christian family life.

Catholic children are encouraged to respect their parents as they are told in the fourth commandment and in Paul's teachings. Parents are encouraged to follow Paul's teachings and treat their children well. Parents are also expected to provide their children with the necessities of life and ensure they are educated and brought up in the Catholic religion. In a mixed marriage (a Catholic married to a non-Catholic), the non-Catholic partner is encouraged to agree that the children have a Catholic upbringing to prevent any division within the family.

Catholics are expected to ensure that their children:
* are baptised (at which time the parents promise to give the children a Catholic upbringing);
* go to Mass on Sunday;
* receive their first communion;
* go to a Catholic school;
* are confirmed.

Catholic children are expected to care for their parents when they are no longer capable of caring for themselves. This is based on the fourth commandment and the teachings of Jesus. He taught that children should not use their gifts to the Temple to ignore their obligations to their elderly parents.

> The family is the *original cell of social life*. It is the natural society in which husband and wife are called to give themselves in love and in the gift of life. Authority, stability and a life of relationships within the family constitute the foundations for freedom, security, and fraternity within society. The family is the community in which, from childhood, one can learn moral values, begin to honour God and make good use of freedom. Family life is an initiation into life in society.

Catechism of the Catholic Church (2207).

> The fourth commandment reminds grown children of their *responsibilities towards their parents*. As much as they can, they must give them material and moral support in old age and in times of illness, loneliness, or distress.

Catechism of the Catholic Church (2218).

How the Church helps with the upbringing of children

The Catholic Church helps parents to bring up their children.

- Catholic schools provide Catholic education and worship in addition to the standard education. (The school buildings are provided and maintained by the Church. The teachers and equipment are paid for by the state.)
- The Church welcomes and provides facilities for families at Mass.
- Classes are given to prepare children for first communion and confirmation.
- Some churches run Children's Liturgies to give children a more Catholic education and to allow parents to be at Mass without the distraction of children.
- Some Catholic churches also run youth clubs and youth activities so that children are helped off the streets and away from bad influences.
- The Catholic Church also provides charities to help family life, e.g. Catholic Marriage Care, the National Catholic Child Welfare Council.

Catholics believe all children have a right to family life, so married couples who cannot have children are encouraged to adopt unwanted children. Each Catholic diocese has a Children's Society to encourage Catholic families to foster children in care.

This girl is dressed in white for her first communion.

The priest blesses the children before they attend the Children's Liturgy.

FACTFILE 36

CHRISTIAN ATTITUDES TO HOMOSEXUALITY

The number of men and women who have deep-seated homosexual tendencies is not negligible. They do not choose their homosexual condition; for most of them it is a trial. They must be accepted with respect, compassion, sensitivity ...

Homosexual persons are called to chastity. By the virtues of self-mastery that teach them inner freedom, at times by the support of disinterested friendship, by prayer and sacramental grace, they can and should gradually and resolutely approach Christian perfection.

Catechism of the Catholic Church (2358-9).

I think I might be gay but I'm not sure about my friend. I love him very much, but I don't have the guts to tell him in case he's straight. I value our friendship and I don't want to risk losing it.

Homosexuality is sexual attraction (often called orientation) to the same sex. **Heterosexuality** refers to sexual attraction to the opposite sex. The Bible condemns homosexuality and at various times in history homosexuality has been a criminal offence (though it was highly regarded by the ancient Greeks). In most western countries homosexual acts between consenting adults are now legal.

As psychology has developed over the past fifty years, it has become clear that at least 5% of the population is homosexual. Most psychologists now agree that homosexuals do not choose to be homosexual and that homosexuality may have genetic cause.

The teaching of the Catholic Church

The Catholic Church accepts that there are homosexuals and that they cannot change their sexual orientation. Therefore, it teaches that:
- homosexual orientation is not a sin and is not to be condemned;
- homosexual activity is a sin and God calls homosexuals to chastity (not to act out their sexual feelings);
- homosexuals will find help from God through the sacraments;
- the Catholic Church offers help to homosexual persons living in accordance with these teachings through organisations such as EnCourage (listed in the Catholic Directory);
- Catholics must respect homosexuals and give them equal treatment and must fight any form of discrimination against them.

The attitudes of other Christians

There are several different attitudes to homosexuality amongst non-Catholic Christians.
- Many conservative Protestants base themselves on biblical teaching and agree with the Catholic attitude.
- Some fundamentalist Protestants believe homosexual orientation is a sin which can be cured by prayer and the power of the Holy Spirit.
- The Church of England and many liberal Protestants teach that lifelong homosexual relationships are acceptable, but are not to be regarded as on a par with heterosexual activity.
- All British Churches teach that any clergy who have a homosexual orientation must not indulge in sexual activity.
- Some Christians (e.g. the Quakers) are moving towards the view that Christian attitudes to homosexuals should be the same as those towards heterosexuals. This would mean homosexual marriages in church. It would also mean homosexuals limiting their sexual activity to one lifelong partner within a homosexual 'marriage'.

We do not reject those who believe that they have more hope of growing in love for God and neighbour with the help of a loving and faithful homophile relationship.

Church of England Report on Homosexuality.

QUESTIONS

Factfile 33 Social Facts on Marriage, Divorce and Family Life

1 What is cohabitation and is it becoming more popular?

2 What is the difference between cohabitation and marriage?

3 Why might some people say serial monogamy is not much different from promiscuity?

4 What evidence is there that marriage is becoming less popular?

5 Why was there a large increase in divorce between 1961 and 1981?

6 What evidence is there that there has been a large increase in one-parent families?

7 Give three reasons why divorce might not be a good idea.

Factfile 34 Christian Teaching on Marriage and Divorce

1 Have a class discussion on why the Catholic Church is against sex before marriage.

2 Using the quotations from the rite of marriage and the *Catechism*, explain how a Catholic marriage service can help a marriage to work.

3 Have a classroom discussion on why the Catholic Church does not allow divorce.

4 "Having a religious wedding ceremony makes no difference to how the marriage works out." Do you agree? Give reasons for your answer showing you have considered another point of view.

Factfile 35 Catholic Teaching on the Family

1 Give three reasons why Catholics regard the family as important.

2 Describe three ways in which Catholicism helps a family to stay together.

3 Write down four ways in which the Church helps with the upbringing of children.

4 Discuss whether a family is more likely to stay together if the parents are Catholic.

Factfile 36 Christian Attitudes to Homosexuality

1 What is homosexuality?

2 Explain how Catholics should treat homosexuals.

10 SOCIAL HARMONY

FACTFILE 37

THE ROLE OF MEN AND WOMEN

Women in the UK have always had the right to own property and earn their own living, but they did not have the same rights as men. When women married, their husbands had the right to use their property. During the second half of the nineteenth century it became the accepted view that married women should stay at home and look after the children (in 1850 about 50% of married women had been in employment, by 1900 it was down to about 15%). The two World Wars (when women had to do men's jobs and did them very well), and the various women's movements for equal rights for women have changed the attitude to the roles of men and women in the UK and it is now generally accepted that men and women are equal.

TABLE 1 WOMEN'S RIGHTS

1882 – The Married Women's Property Act allowed married women to keep their property separate from their husband's.

1892 – The Local Government Act allowed women the vote in local elections and the right to stand as councillors.

1918 – The Representation of the People Act allowed women over 31 to vote in parliamentary elections (men could vote at 21).

1928 – Electoral Reform Act gave the vote to women over 21 and allowed women to stand as MP's.

1970 – The Equal Pay Act required employers to give women the same pay as men – equal pay for like work regardless of the employee's sex.

1975 – Sex Discrimination Act made it illegal to discriminate in jobs on grounds of sex or whether a person is married.

TABLE 2 EMPLOYMENT BY GENDER

| | Males (thousands) | | Females (thousands) | |
	Full-time	Part-time	Full-time	Part-time
1984	13,240	570	5,422	4,343
1989	14,071	734	6,336	4,907
1994	12,875	998	6,131	5,257

In 1970 women's earnings were 63.1% of men's. By 1985 they were 74.1% of men's.

Source: Social Trends 25.

Biblical teachings and the roles of men and women

The Bible was written when society was patriarchal, i.e. men had more power than women, and so much Biblical teaching gives the dominant role in life to men. Christian attitudes to the roles of men and women have changed, and continue to change, during the twentieth century. Even many of those who still accept the Biblical teaching think it needs re-interpreting.

There is, however, evidence from the Gospels that Jesus treated women as equals. He preached in the court of women in the Jerusalem temple (*Matthew* 21:23-22:14). He treated a Samaritan woman as his equal (*John* 4). He had women disciples who stayed with him at the cross (*Matthew* 27:55, *Mark* 15:40-41, *Luke* 23:27, *John* 25:27) unlike the male disciples who ran away. It was to the women that Jesus first appeared after his resurrection.

> God created man in the image of himself, in the image of God he created him, male and female he created them.

Genesis 1:27.

> I urge Euodia, and I urge Syntyche to come to agreement with each other in the Lord; and I ask you, Syzygus, really to be a 'partner' and help them. These women have struggled hard for the gospel with me, along with Clement and all my other fellow workers, whose names are written in the book of life.

Philippians 4:2-3.

> Be subject to one another out of reverence for Christ. Wives should be subject to their husbands as to the Lord, since, as Christ is the head of the Church and saves the whole body, so is a husband the head of his wife; and as the Church is subject to Christ, so should wives be to their husbands, in everything ... To sum up: you also, each one of you, must love his wife as he loves himself; and let every wife respect her husband.

Ephesians 5:22-24, 33.

> There is neither Jew nor Greek, slave nor free, male nor female, for you are all one in Christ.

Galatians 3:28.

'The Mourning of Christ' by Sandro Botticelli.

Catholic teaching on the roles of men and women

The Catholic Church teaches that men and women should have equal roles in life.

On the basis of *Genesis* 1:27, the Church teaches that men and women have equal status in the sight of God. In the new Roman Catholic marriage service, the priest says: 'May her husband put his trust in her and recognise that she is his equal and the heir with him to the life of grace.'

The Church teaches that women should have equal rights in society and has campaigned against unfair treatment of women around the world. In its 1971 report, 'Justice in the World', the Third World Synod of Bishops called for women to 'participate in, and share responsibility for, the life of society and of the Church.'

The *Catholic Encyclopaedia* states that in the USA 'women comprise over 80% of those who minister as teachers and sponsors of the catechumenate and who serve the poor, visit the sick, and comfort the grieving. Half of parish council members, lectors and eucharistic ministers are women.'

In Catholic teaching women have all the same rights as men and are able to study and teach in theological colleges.

> Men and women have been *created*, which is to say, *willed* by God: on the one hand, in perfect equality as human persons; on the other, in their respective beings as man and woman.

Catechism of the Catholic Church (369).

> In November 1994, the US bishops approved a pastoral reflection on women in the Church and in society, 'Strengthening the Bonds of Peace', which rejects sexism in Church teaching and practice and commits the bishops to enhance the participation of women in every possible aspect of church life.

Catholic Encyclopaedia.

Different attitudes to the role of women in ministry

The Catholic Church accepts that women can fulfil every function in the Catholic Church except that of deacon, priest and bishop.

Women can be hospital and college chaplains; they can, and do teach, in theological colleges and seminaries; they can teach candidates for confirmation; and they can be lectors and eucharistic ministers. In some parts of the world, they are even licensed by the bishop to carry out baptisms, weddings, and funerals because of a shortage of priests.

However, the Church teaches that only men can be ordained:

> The Lord Jesus chose men ... to form the college of the twelve apostles, and the apostles did the same when they chose collaborators to succeed them in their ministry ... For this reason the ordination of women is not possible.

Catechism of the Catholic Church (1577).

All Orthodox churches accept this teaching and do not allow women priests because the priest is representing Jesus at the Eucharist.

Some Church of England priests have left to become Catholics since the Church of England decided to ordain women. They believe that the Church of England did not have the authority to make this decision, because it contradicted Jesus' choice of men as his spostles and the unbroken Catholic tradition of ordaining only men.

Some fundamentalist Protestant Churches do not allow women to lead services because of St Paul's teaching in *1 Timothy* that women should be silent in church.

Although the Catholic Church does not allow women to become priests, it insists that they are treated with full human dignity alongside men in both public and domestic life. Pope John XXIII said in *Pacem et Terris* 1963:

> Since women are becoming ever more conscious of their human dignity, they will not tolerate being treated as mere material instruments, but demand rights befitting a human person both in domestic and public life.

The United Reformed Church, the Methodist Church, the Church of England and most Protestant churches have complete equality for women in the Church's ministry because they believe that both men and women were created in the image of God, therefore both can be ministers. They point to the many women who followed Jesus and say that the only reason Jesus appointed men as his apostles was because of the culture of his day. If he had been alive today, he would have had women apostles.

Women deacons wait to be ordained priests in the Church of England by the Bishop Barry Rogers, Bristol.

THE UK AS A MULTI-ETHNIC SOCIETY

Social factors

The UK has always been a mixed society – Celts, Romans, Angles, Saxons, Jutes, Danes, Vikings, Normans are all ancestors of the English.

The UK has always believed in human freedom and offered asylum to those suffering persecution – to French Protestants (Huguenots) in the seventeenth century, to Russian Jews in the nineteenth century, to European Jews escaping Hitler in the 1930's.

In the nineteenth century the UK built up an overseas empire around the world. In exchange for being ruled by Britain, citizens of the Empire were allowed to settle in the UK. Slaves who set foot on English soil immediately became free. As a result, small black communities grew up in Bristol, Liverpool and Cardiff.

The Empire became known as the Commonwealth as nations gained their independence from the UK. In the 1950s there was substantial immigration from the Commonwealth. People came from India, Pakistan, Bangladesh, West Africa and the Caribbean to lessen a labour shortage in the UK. Many of these workers had fought for the UK in the Second World War (more people fought from the Commonwealth than from the UK itself).

British Asians.

TABLE 1 ETHNIC MINORITIES IN THE UK 1991
Indian 787,000
Afro-Caribbean 495,000
European/Australian 472,000
Pakistani 428,000
Mixed 287,000
Chinese 125,000
African 112,000
Bangladeshi 108,000

Source: Race in the 90s, CRE.

In 1991 4.8% of the UK's population was ethnic minority and 50% of these were born in the UK.

Meena, a young Asian woman with 8 GCSE's and 3 A levels, went for an interview at an insurance firm where her friend, Sally, worked.

I didn't get the job. But Sally told me they said that, in the recession, it was important to give jobs to your own. Now tell me, what does that mean? I was born here, I speak with a brummie accent.

My grandfather, like so many others, died fighting for this country – he was in Italy – we even have a letter from his commander about how brave he was.

My mother works in the health service, my father in insurance. They've never collected a penny in benefits, and have paid taxes for twenty five years. Dad won't even let me go on the dole. So what does 'your own' mean ?

Source: Race through the 90s, CRE.

RACIAL PREJUDICE – THINKING CERTAIN RACES ARE INFERIOR OR SUPERIOR, USUALLY WITHOUT EVIDENCE.

RACIAL DISCRIMINATION – PUTTING PREJUDICE INTO PRACTICE AND TREATING PEOPLE LESS FAVOURABLY BECAUSE OF THEIR RACIAL, NATIONAL, ETHNIC OR COLOUR ORIGINS.

RACISM – THE BELIEF THAT SOME RACES ARE SUPERIOR TO OTHERS, BASED ON SUPPOSED BIOLOGICAL FACTS.

The Commission for Racial Equality was set up by the Government in 1976 to enforce the Race Relations Act. It has three duties:

- to fight against racial discrimination;

- to make people understand the importance of giving everyone an equal chance, whatever their race, colour, ethnic origin or nationality;

- to keep a check on how the law is working, and tell the Government how it could be improved.

THE RACE RELATIONS ACT 1976

- makes it unlawful to discriminate against anyone because of race, colour, nationality, ethnic or national origins in the sphere of jobs, training, housing, education and the provision of services;

- makes it unlawful to use threatening or abusive or insulting words in public which could stir up racial hatred;

- makes it illegal to publish anything likely to cause racial hatred.

'I believe deeply that all men and women should be able to go as far as talent, ambition and effort can take them. There should be no barriers of background, no barriers of religion, no barriers of race. I want ... a society that encourages each and every one to fulfil his or her potential to the utmost ... let me say here and now that I regard any barrier built on race to be pernicious ...'

Speech by Prime Minister John Major, September 1991.

TABLE 2 UNEMPLOYMENT RATES BY ETHNIC GROUP SPRING 1994

White	8%
Indian	15%
Chinese/other ethnic groups/ mixed race	19%
Black (West Indian and African)	26%
Pakistani/Bangladeshi	28%

RACIAL ATTACKS REPORTED TO THE POLICE

	1988	1990
England and Wales	4383	6459
Scotland	299	636

Source: Social Trends in the 90s, CRE.

Catholic teaching on racial harmony

The New Testament is clearly opposed to racism – Jesus treated a Samaritan woman as his equal (*John* 4), healed a Roman centurion's servant (*Luke* 7) and had a man from Africa helping him to carry his cross (*Luke* 23:28).

After a vision from God, Peter said:

"I now really understand ... that God has no favourites, but that anybody of any nationality who fears him and does what is right is acceptable to him."

Acts 10:34.

Paul said:

"From one one single principle he not only created the whole human race so that they could occupy the entire earth, but he decreed the times and limits of their habitation."

Acts 17:26.

For all of you are the children of God, through faith, in Christ Jesus, since every one of you that has been baptised has been clothed in Christ. There can be neither Jew nor Greek, there can be neither slave nor freeman, there can be neither male nor female – for you are all one in Christ Jesus.

Galatians 3:26-28.

The ultimate source for Christian teaching on racial harmony is the parable of the Good Samaritan where Jesus showed that races who hated each other should be loving and caring for each other if they were following God's command to 'Love your neighbour as yourself.' (*Luke* 10:25-37.)

The Catholic Church is firmly committed to racial harmony. There are Catholic cardinals and bishops of every race and colour of skin and the Church is dedicated to fighting racism in all its forms.

Created in the image of the one God and equally endowed with rational souls, all men have the same nature and the same origin. Redeemed by the sacrifice of Christ, all are called to participate in the same divine beatitude: all therefore enjoy an equal dignity ... Every form of social or cultural discrimination in fundamental personal rights on the grounds of sex, race, colour, social conditions, language or religion, must be curbed and eradicated as incompatible with God's design.

Catechism of the Catholic Church (1934-35).

Martin Luther King and racial harmony

Martin Luther King was born in Atlanta in 1929. He was the son of a Baptist minister and after studying theology at university he became a minister too.

At university he studied Mahatma Gandhi's idea of *satyagraha* (if what you fight for is true, and you use non-violent methods, eventually your case will overcome your opponents').

King became minister of the Baptist Church in Montgomery, Alabama, and was soon leading the black civil rights movement. In many of the southern United States at this time, black people were denied their civil rights to equal treatment, equal education and the right to vote. In many places, blacks were kept apart from whites. In Montgomery, there were 'whites only' seats on the buses. An old black woman sat on one of the these and was arrested. This led to a threat of violence from black people in Montgomery. Martin Luther KIng was chairman of the Montgomery Improvement Society and he decided to fight against segregation on the buses, but declared, 'We will not resort to violence. We will not degrade ourselves with hatred. Love will be returned for hate.'

So instead of fighting, he organised a boycott of the buses. After 382 days the US Supreme Court ruled that state laws imposing segregation were unconstitutional. King then began the Civil Rights Movement to give black Americans equal rights with white Americans. He insisted that it be a non-violent movement and was made to suffer for this. He was frequently arrested and jailed and often beaten up, but he refused to resort to violence. In 1963, a black church was bombed when King led a march to stop segregation in shops and hotels. The bomb killed four young girls who were at Sunday School and shocked America. When King called a march on Washington in August, 1963, in support of civil rights legislation, over 250,000 Americans of all colours and religions joined in and the legislation was passed.

In 1964, at the age of 36, King was given the Nobel Peace Prize, the youngest person ever to receive it. He continued his non-violent campaign to bring social harmony between America's black and white communities, but like his hero, Gandhi, he was assassinated by a violent opponent in April, 1968.

Although King was influenced by Gandhi, his chief influence was Jesus. King was a Christian and it was his reading of the Sermon on the Mount and the parable of the sheep and the goats that convinced him that all people should be treated equally and that the way to achieve this was by 'turning the other cheek' as Jesus commanded.

I have a dream that my children will one day live in a nation where they will not be judged by the colour of their skin but by the sort of persons they are. I have a dream that one day all God's children, black men, white men, Jews and Gentiles, Protestants and Catholics, will be able to join hands and sing in the words of the black people's old song, 'free at last, thank God almighty, we are free at last.'

Martin Luther King's speech at the end of the march on Washington.

The call for a worldwide fellowship that lifts neighbourly concern beyond one's tribe, race, class and nation is in reality a call for an all-embracing and unconditional love for all men ... We can no longer afford to worship the God of hate or bow before the altar of retaliation.

'Chaos or Community', Martin Luther King.

FACTFILE 39

THE UK AS A MULTI-FAITH SOCIETY

MULTI-FAITH SOCIETY – MANY DIFFERENT RELIGIONS IN ONE SOCIETY.

RELIGIOUS PLURALISM – ACCEPTING ALL FAITHS AS HAVING AN EQUAL RIGHT TO CO-EXIST.

Many societies were mono-faith (having only one religion) societies until the twentieth century.

In some ways, Great Britain has been a multi-faith society ever since the Reformation in the sixteenth century. Although Queen Elizabeth I made the Church of England the state religion, there were other Churches: Protestants who were not Church of England (Nonconformists), Roman Catholics, and from 1657, Jews. So Britain had to have laws encouraging **religious toleration** (everyone is free to follow their chosen religion without discrimination).

However, it was in the twentieth century that Great Britain became truly multi-faith as members of non-Christian religions came to Britain as immigrants (although immigrants from the Caribbean and Africa were mainly Christian).

How Britain Legally Became a Religiously Plural Society

1671   Heresy ceased to be a crime.

1688   Nonconformists were given freedom of worship.

1828   Nonconformists were given the same political rights as members of the Church of England.

1829   Roman Catholics were given the same political rights as members of the Church of England.

1858   Jews were given the same political rights as members of the Church of England.

This meant that members of any religion were free to worship in Great Britain and had equal political rights.

A Hindu temple in North London.

Religious statistics for the UK

These statistics are based on *The UK Christian Handbook 1988* and the Central Office of Information *Aspects of Britain – Religion 1992*.

It is very difficult to compare statistics of membership because some religions count people as members if they are born into the religion, therefore these figures are based on people who claim some form of allegiance to the religion.

CHRISTIANITY –	Church of England 25 million Nonconformists 5.7 million Roman Catholics 5.7 million number of churches 50,800
ISLAM –	between 600,000 (*UK Christian Handbook*) and 1 million (*Aspects of Britain*) number of mosques 600
JUDAISM –	111,000 (*UK Handbook*) 300,000 (*Aspects of Britain*) number of synagogues 356
HINDUISM –	155,000 (*UK Handbook*) 300,000 (*Aspects of Britain*) number of mandirs 150
SIKHISM –	150,000 (*UK Handbook*) 300,000 (*Aspects of Britain*) number of gurdwaras 160
BUDDHISM –	25,000 (*UK Handbook*) no figure in *Aspects of Britain* number of monasteries and other buildings 200+

The Catholic Church and other religions

The Catholic Church believes in religious freedom, that is, it believes that everyone has the right to follow, or not follow, any religion they wish. It also believes that Christianity is the only religion with the complete truth and that it has a missionary duty to preach Christianity to all nations.

The problem in a multi-faith society is, 'Should Christians try to bring members of other faiths into Christianity, or should all religions live side by side seeking God in their own ways?' The Catholic Church believes it is possible to do both, but most important is not to discriminate against people because of their religion. The Church recognises that while it is the Catholic Church which has the true revelation from God, people can come to God by other paths.

> "Go, therefore, make disciples of all nations, baptise them in the name of the Father and of the Son and of the Holy Spirit, and teach them to observe all the commandments I gave you. And look, I am always with you until the end of time."

All nations form but one community. This is so because all stem from the one stock which God created to people the entire earth, and also because all share a common destiny, namely God ... The Catholic Church recognises in other religions that search ... for the God who is unknown yet near since he gives life and breath and all things and wants all men to be saved.

Catechism of the Catholic Church (842-43).

Matthew 28:19-20.

> Although in ways known only to himself God can lead those who, through no fault of their own, are ignorant of the Gospel, to that faith without which it is impossible to please him, the Church still has the obligation and also the sacred right to evangelise all men.

Catechism of the Catholic Church (848).

Religions working together

The different churches have worked together for many years. In 1990 the Council of Churches for Britain and Ireland was established. It includes all the major Churches (there are 30 member churches) and meets twice a year. England, Wales, Scotland and Ireland have their own groups which are organised in every town as Churches Together.

The Council of Christians and Jews has existed since the Second World War to promote better understanding between the two religions and to prevent religious and racial bitterness.

The Inter-faith Network for the United Kingdom represents Buddhists, Christians, Hindus, Jains, Jews, Muslims and Sikhs. It works for increased tolerance and understanding and tries to encourage harmony by concentrating on what the religions have in common rather than on what divides them.

Many cities have their own groups to help the different religions in their cities get along. In Glasgow, for example, the Sharing of Faiths movement was founded in the 1970s by Christians, Jews, Muslims, Hindus and Sikhs. It meets on a monthly basis and has an annual presentation in the city centre with stalls explaining each religion to the people of Glasgow. Its aim is sharing so that people will realise that each of these religions is a way of finding God and a purpose in life.

FACTFILE 40

WAR AND PEACE

Catholic teaching as outlined by Popes Leo XII, John XXIII, Paul VI and John Paul II is that all Christians should seek to establish peace in the world. They link peace with justice and teach that Christians should try to achieve peace by removing the injustice and greed which cause war.

For Catholics, injustice includes:
- not giving equal rights to all races and religions;
- not sharing wealth fairly;
- not respecting a country's borders;
- not respecting democratically agreed decisions.

It is possible to look at any conflict and see that its origins lie in injustice (e.g. Arab-Israeli, Northern Ireland, Bosnia).

In the event of their country being involved in war, Catholics have two options permitted by the Church. Both aim to bring about peace.

A United Nations soldier and an unidentified woman give first aid to a Bosnian soldier wounded by a sniper.

Just War

Catholics may fight in a just war as defined in the teachings of St Thomas Aquinas. They may fight if:

- the cause of war is just (resisting aggression or removing great injustice);
- the war is being fought by the authority of a government or the United Nations;
- it is done with the intention of restoring peace;
- they do so as a last resort – all non-violent ways have been tried and failed;
- they have a reasonable chance of success;
- the methods used avoid killing innocent civilians – military personnel could use the doctrine of double effect, e.g. they are not guilty if a bomb aimed at an armaments factory hits a hospital;
- the methods used are proportional to the cause – weapons of mass destruction would seem to be banned; you can't wipe out the world because someone attacks a small offshore island.

Pacifism

This is the view that war can never be justified for a Christian. It is based on Jesus' teaching in the Sermon on the Mount about turning the other cheek, and his refusal to defend himself when he was arrested. Catholic pacifists believe that the only way to achieve peace is to refuse to be involved in war. The Catholic Church has a large international pacifist group called Pax Christi which is very active in the UK and the USA. There were more Catholic **conscientious objectors** (people who refuse to fight on principle when conscripted) in the Vietnam War than any other religious group. The Catholic bishops of the USA were the only religious leaders to condemn the Vietnam war as unjust.

The Catholic Church teaches that Catholics can use either the just war or pacifism as a way of bringing peace.

The fifth commandment forbids the intentional destruction of human life. Because of the evils and injustices that accompany all war, the Church insistently urges everyone to prayer and to action so that the divine Goodness may free us from the ancient bondage of war. All citizens and all governments are obliged to work for the avoidance of war.

However, 'as long as the danger of war persists and there is no international authority with the necessary competence and power, governments cannot be denied the right of lawful self-defense, once all peace efforts have failed.'

Catechism of the Catholic Church (2307-8).

QUESTIONS

1 Write down three pieces of evidence which show women have gained more equality in the past 100 years.

2 Have a group discussion on the areas where women still do not receive equal treatment and write down whether boys have different views from girls.

3 "Religion does not give women equal rights." Do you agree? Give reasons for your answer, showing that you have considered another point of view.

Factfile 38 The UK as a Multi-Ethnic Society

1 Write down the following:
a) two pieces of evidence that the UK has always been multi-ethnic;
b) evidence of the proportion of the UK's present day population that belongs to ethnic minorities;
c) the difference between prejudice and discrimination;
d) what the law says about racial discrimination.

2 Write down two biblical and two Church reasons why Christians may work to achieve racial harmony.

3 "All people living in a country should have the same rights whatever their race or religion." Do you agree? Give reasons for your answer showing you have considered another point of view.

4 Explain why Martin Luther King felt he had to stand up for civil rights for American blacks.

Factfiles 39 The UK as a Multi-Faith Society

1 What is the difference between a mono-faith and a multi-faith society?

2 How do religious laws in Britain show it is a multi-faith society?

3 "There should be no attempt to convert people in a multi-faith society." Do you agree? Give reasons for your answer showing you have considered another point of view.

Factfile 40 War and Peace

1 Explain why some Catholics are pacifists.

2 Make a list of the conditions necessary for a Catholic to fight in a just war.

THE CATHOLIC CHURCH AT WORLD LEVEL

11

The word '**catholic**' means universal or worldwide and the Roman Catholic Church is a truly universal Church. There is a diocese of the Catholic Church in almost every country in the world. In 1994 it was estimated that at least 1.75 billion of the world's 5 billion population was Catholic.

Many countries are called Catholic countries because the majority of their population regards itself as Catholic. These countries are:

Argentina, Brazil,
Bolivia, Chile,
Colombia, Costa Rica,
Ecuador, El Salvador,   **South and Central America**
Guatemala, Honduras,
Mexico, Nicaragua,
Panama, Paraguay,
Peru, Uruguay, Venezuela

Belgium, France,
Hungary, Ireland, Italy,   **Europe**
Poland, Portugal,
Spain

Ivory Coast, Zaire   **Africa**

Philippines   **Asia**

Over 70% of Catholics are non-white, non-European.

FACTFILE 41

THE INTERNATIONAL DIMENSION OF THE CHURCH

The Church is catholic because she has been sent out by Christ on a mission to the whole of the human race ... The character of universality which adorns the People of God is a gift from the Lord himself whereby the Catholic Church ceaselessly and efficaciously seeks for the return of all humanity and all its goods, under Christ the Head in the unity of his Spirit.

Catechism of the Catholic Church (831).

Pope John Paul II on his arrival at Veracruz, Mexico.

FACTFILE 42

THE ORGANISATION OF THE CHURCH

A bishop celebrating Mass on Palm Sunday to dedicate a new church building.

The Catholic Church is organised as a hierarchy under the leadership of the Pope. The Pope is the successor of St Peter (who was given special authority by Jesus), and the bishops are the successors of Jesus' other apostles. The supreme authority of the Catholic Church lies in all the bishops (the college of bishops) working with the Pope in an ecumenical council, like Vatican II. The Pope appoints senior bishops as cardinals, some of whom live in Rome. It is the cardinals who take over the running of the Church when the Pope dies and who meet as a college in the Vatican to elect the new Pope.

The Pope is the Bishop of Rome and lives in Vatican City. This was given to him by the Italian government in the nineteenth century and means that the head and the headquarters of the Church are not in any one country. The Pope organises the Church through the Curia which is like a cabinet of cardinals. Each cardinal is responsible for one of the nine congregations of the Church (like government departments). Each congregation is responsible for a different area of the Church, e.g. Faith and Doctrine, Finance. Each cardinal is assisted by seven bishops selected by the Pope from around the world and they serve for five years.

Each bishop is responsible for a diocese and each country usually has a conference of bishops who meet together to decide on Catholic attitudes in their area. Some areas which have a common culture form an ecclesiastical province known as a patriarchate or region. The bishops of these areas can meet together in a synod or provincial council.

In his own diocese, the bishop appoints priests to parishes and is responsible for everything in the diocese including the education system and the marriage tribunals.

It is the Pope and the bishops acting together who exercise the *Magisterium* which teaches the true faith of the Church.

> Helped by the priests, their co-workers, and by the deacons, the bishops have the duty of authentically teaching the faith, celebrating divine worship, above all the Eucharist, and guiding their churches as true pastors. Their responsibility also includes concern for all the Churches with and under the Pope.

Catechism of the Catholic Church (939).

> The Lord made St Peter the visible foundation of his Church. He entrusted the keys of the Church to him. The bishop of the Church of Rome, successor to St Peter, is 'head of the college of bishops, the Vicar of Christ and Pastor of the universal Church on earth'.

Catechism of the Catholic Church (936).

In 1958 Pope Pius XII died. He had been Pope since 1939 and had kept the Church faithful to the decisions of Vatican I, the first council of the Church held in the Vatican, in 1871. This council had rejected many of the changes already happening in the nineteenth century and so, in some ways, the Catholic Church was out of touch with the world of 1958. The new Pope, John XXIII, decided that the Church needed bringing up to date (*aggiornamento*) so that it could preach the Gospel more effectively in the modern world. So he called a new council of all the bishops and approximately 2500 of them from all over the world came to Rome for what became known as Vatican II. It had four sessions: October – December 1962, September – December 1963, September – November 1964, September – December 1965.

Not only was this the largest council ever held, it also represented far more areas of the world and had observers from other Christian Churches.

The decisions of Vatican II

1 Changes to the Liturgy
Before Vatican II, all Catholic liturgies throughout the world were in Latin and Mass was celebrated at the high altar facing in the same direction. When there was more than one priest, each celebrated at his own altar. At communion lay people received only the host and were not offered the chalice.

The bishops at the Council decided that:
- the **vernacular** (the language of the country) could be used in the liturgy;
- the laity may have communion under both kinds (the host and the chalice) on some occasions;
- priests could concelebrate Mass.

2 The Bible
All public readings from the Bible had been in Latin. Vatican II authorised new translations and ordered that the Bible should be read in the vernacular at Mass. There should be a sermon (homily) to explain the meaning of the readings and to relate them to life in the modern world.

3 The nature of the Church
Vatican II declared that the Church is the People of God — not just priests, bishops and pope. It declared that, although the Pope is the head of the Church, all major decisions should be made by the pope and the bishops acting together as the bishops are also successors of the apostles.

Vatican II said that each national Church should have a conference of bishops. It should meet regularly to discuss issues of concern. It also elects representatives to the Synod of Bishops in Rome which the Pope should call at regular intervals to discuss issues with him.

THE REFORMS OF VATICAN II

It is the goal of this most sacred Council to intensify the growth of Catholics in Christian living; to make more responsive to the requirements of our times those Church observances which are open to adaptation ... Hence the Council has special reasons for judging it a duty to provide for the renewal and fostering of the liturgy.

Introduction to the Constitution on the Sacred Liturgy, from 'Documents of Vatican II'.

4 The Clergy

After a close vote, the Council decided that only celibate men should be ordained as priests (except for the married clergy already allowed by the Eastern Rite – Orthodox Christians who reunited with Rome after the Great Schism of 1054). It decided that married men be ordained into the **permanent diaconate** (a lower order of ordained persons who can do everything except celebrate the Eucharist and pronounce absolution). It also urged bishops to appoint lay ministers to help with pastoral work and services.

Vatican II urged all bishops to appoint a synod of the priests in their diocese to advise them on diocesan affairs.

The religious orders (monks and nuns) were told to look again at the reasons for their foundation and to revise their way of living so as to challenge the modern world as they challenged the times in which they were originally established.

5 The Church and the world

Vatican II stated that the Church has to be concerned with the world and so it:

- opposed all divisions based on race, sex or class;
- condemned the arms race;
- emphasised the solidarity of the Catholic Church with the poor and oppressed;
- set up a media secretariat;
- agreed that Catholics have a right to limit the size of their families, but left it to a Papal Commission to decide how.

Vatican II also made decisions on the Church's missionary activity, Christian education, and relationships with non-Christians.

A lay missionary in Ethiopia, working as a teacher.

Relations with other Churches

Vatican II totally transformed the attitude of the Catholic Church to other Christian Churches.

In 1920, Pope Pius XI had issued an encyclical claiming that the Roman Catholic Church is the only true Church, and that people could only be saved if they joined it.

The Vatican II documents on ecumenism, the Eastern Catholic Churches and religious liberty made the following changes:
1 The Church includes all Christians and is not limited to Catholics.
2 God uses the other Christian Churches in offering salvation to all mankind.
3 The Catholic Church is not the only means to salvation.
4 Both Catholics and Protestants were responsible for the mistakes of the Reformation.
5 There should be religious freedom. No one should be forced to believe and non-Catholics must be given equal rights in Catholic countries.
6 It is the duty of all Christians to seek common ground with other faiths and not allow religious intolerance or persecution.
7 The excommunication of the Patriarch of Constantinople was revoked, so ending a source of bitterness between Catholic and Orthodox Churches.
8 It stated that it is the duty of all Catholics to work with the Ecumenical Movement and set up the Secretariat for Christian Unity.

> Christians should also work together in the use of every possible means to relieve the afflictions of our times such as famine and natural disasters, illiteracy and poverty, lack of housing and the unequal distribution of wealth. Through such cooperation, all believers in Christ are able to learn easily how they can understand each other better and esteem each other more, and how the road to the unity of Christians may be made smooth.

Decree on Ecumenism, 'Documents of Vatican II'.

Pope John Paul II and Archbishop Robert Runcie pray together in Canterbury Cathedral in 1982, the first time a Pope had visited England since the Reformation.

FACTFILE 44

SUBSEQUENT DEVELOPMENTS

Many of the decisions of Vatican II were carried out during the pontificate of Paul VI (1963-1978).

New rites for Mass and other ceremonies were introduced and used mainly in local languages (the vernacular).

A new translation of the Bible into English, *The Jerusalem Bible*, was published in 1965.

In most churches the altar was moved nearer to the people.

Paul VI formed the synod of bishops in Rome and national Churches formed their own conferences of bishops.

Many bishops formed synods of priests in their diocese.

The Vatican sends observers to the World Council of Churches.

The Catholic Church in England and Wales became a member of Churches Together which links most Christian Churches.

The Catholic Church has permanent deacons and lay eucharistic ministers who can be married.

The Church has made statements on justice, poverty, racism, peace, world hunger and debt showing its concern for the needs of the world.

New papal secretariats have been established to deal with Christian Unity, the Media, Justice and Peace, other faiths and non-believers.

Pope Paul VI slowed down some reforms as he became concerned that the Church might be moving too far too fast. His encyclical *'Humanae Vitae'* reaffirmed the Church's traditional teaching on contraception.

Lay eucharistic ministers taking part at a Mass on Palm Sunday.

The pontificate of John Paul II

Karol Wojtyla was the first non-Italian Pope since Hadrian VI in 1523 and the youngest Pope since Pius IX in 1846. He became John Paul II.

John Paul had spent almost all his priestly life under communist rule and believed that the collapse of the communist Soviet Empire was achieved by the spiritual superiority of Christianity. It seems that on becoming pope he was upset to find divisions among Catholics about the reforms of Vatican II and he felt it was his duty to make the Church in the Western world the force it had been in the communist world. He felt the Church needed a clear identity with good discipline so that it would speak to the world with one voice. To do this Pope John Paul II has:

* emphasised his role of leadership in the Church;
* emphasised that all Catholics must hold to the traditional teaching of the Church;
* tried to unite the Church by visiting 123 countries;
* authorised a new catechism of the Church to set out Catholic beliefs clearly;
* reaffirmed Catholic traditions such as the role of the Blessed Virgin Mary, celibacy of the clergy, no contraception, no abortion, and that homosexual acts are wrong.

John Paul II has maintained the ideas of Vatican II but made sure they were not extended so that the Catholic Church can be seen as part of the modern world yet true to its duty to preserve the faith handed down from Jesus through the apostles and Popes.

Pope John Paul II arrives in Great Britain, 1982. The Pope has visited 123 countries in his efforts to unite the Church. In his traditional gesture, he kisses the ground on his arrival in a foreign country.

QUESTIONS

Factfile 41 The International Dimension of the Catholic Church

1 How many Catholics are there in the world?

2 Name a Catholic country in each of the four continents (Africa, Asia, America, Europe).

3 Why are there Catholics all over the world?

Factfile 42 The Organisation of the Church

1 Give three different titles for the Pope.

2 How is the headquarters of the Catholic Church organised?

3 How is the Catholic Church organised in a country?

Factfile 43 The Reforms of Vatican II

1 Make a list of the main decisions of Vatican II.

2 Which do you think were the most important decisions and why?

Factfiles 44 Subsequent Developments

1 "Vatican II is the best thing that ever happened to the Catholic Church." Do you agree? Give reasons for your answer, showing you have considered another point of view.

THE RELIGIOUS LIFE

12

Vocation

Vocation comes from a Latin word meaning calling. Christians believe that they have a calling. They have been called by God to be followers of Jesus, to be members of the Church and to make their pilgrimage on earth. In the Old Testament God calls people directly by speaking to them and telling them what to do. He also speaks indirectly through people's experience of life, or through natural or historical events. The Gospels indicate that a decisive event for Jesus took place through his meeting with John the Baptist. He heard the voice of God calling him his Son, he received the Holy Spirit and then he began his public ministry. Jesus in turn called his disciples who were to join him in the proclamation of the Gospel and in the establishment of God's kingdom.

Varieties

As well as the common vocation of all Christians there is also the personal call to a specific state of life. A person could be called to married life and parenthood or to celibacy and the religious life. A vocation could be realised through one's employment, say as a nurse or teacher, especially if it gave the person the opportunity to show and share God's love in the lives of others. But what a person does may be less important than how and why a person does it. Vocation has nothing to do with the pursuit of money or fame or power for oneself. Vocation is measured by how much one gives not how much one gets. It was the tradition before Vatican II for Catholics to limit vocation to those called to the sacramental ministry or religious life. It was also assumed that such people were spiritually superior. Nowadays no vocation is regarded as more important than another.

> There are many different gifts, but it is always the same Spirit; there are many different ways of serving, but it is always the same Lord. There are many different forms of activity, but in everybody it is the same God who is at work in them all. The particular manifestation of the Spirit granted to each one is to be used for the general good.

1 Corinthians 12:4-7.

The Church and the world need people to use their gifts in the service of God in a variety of different ways.

FACTFILE 45

CHRISTIAN VOCATION

> It was at this time that Jesus came from Nazareth in Galilee and was baptised in the Jordan by John. And at once, as he was coming up out of the water, he saw the heavens torn apart and the Spirit, like a dove, descending on him. And a voice came from heaven, "You are my Son, the Beloved; my favour rests on you."

Mark 1:9-11.

As he was walking along the Lake of Galilee he saw Simon and Simon's brother Andrew casting a net in the lake – for they were fishermen. And Jesus said to them "Come after me and I will make you fishers of people." And at once they left their nets and followed him.
Going on a little further, he saw James son of Zebedee and his brother John; they too were in their boat, mending the nets. At once he called them and, leaving their father Zebedee in the boat with the men he employed, they went after him.

Mark 1:16-20.

He called the people and his disciples to him and said, "If anyone wants to be a follower of mine, let him renounce himself and take up his cross and follow me. Anyone who wants to save his life will lose it; but anyone who loses his life for my sake, and for the sake of the Gospel, will save it. What gain, then, is it for anyone to win the whole world and forfeit his life? And indeed what can anyone offer in exchange for his life?"

Mark 9:34-37.

Discipleship

Discipleship comes from a Latin word meaning learner. Jesus was a teacher and his first followers learned from him. Jesus chose his disciples to learn how to be his followers and how to give their lives in the service of others. He warned them that like him they had to be willing to die and that to find life they had to be willing to lose it. He told them that to be a disciple required learning not only from his teaching but also from his example. Being a disciple meant new beliefs, new values and a completely different way of life in which apparent success could be failure and apparent failure could be true success. Love, compassion and service are the marks of a disciple of Jesus. On the night before he died he was full of sorrow but showed by his prayer to his Father that he would do whatever was God's will. Those who pay the cost of discipleship like Jesus will share his reward.

Witness

Christians are called to be witnesses to the love of God, to their faith in Jesus and to the power of the Holy Spirit in their lives. To be a **witness** is to give evidence in public and by doing so to attract others to the Christian way of life. The first Christians did this and their faith spread throughout the world because of it. Some were called like Jesus to give their lives. These people are called **martyrs**. Martyr comes from the Greek word meaning witness. Few Christians nowadays are called to be martyrs but all can be witnesses through their daily life and work. Some Christians are called to witness through the ministry or in missionary work. Others have opportunities in the family and through friendships in the Church and at work. Ordinary Christians can witness by giving time and money to support good causes or through involvement in politics. Like Jesus, they can teach by the example of their lives.

Communities

During the first three centuries Christians were subject to a series of systematic persecutions. To be a faithful Christian meant to be willing to be a martyr. This required a high level of dedication to the gospel. All Christians would know others who like Jesus had paid the supreme sacrifice. When Christianity came into favour and the persecutions stopped some Christians wanted to restore the high level of dedication. To do this they went into the desert to live as hermits. They then joined together in communities. This was the beginning of monastic life. **Monasteries** are communities of Christians who have separated themselves from worldly life to commit themselves to become as perfect Christians as possible. Such people are called monks or nuns and they live under an arrangement called a **rule**. The best known monastic rule is the rule of Saint Benedict. Religious communities are now more diverse in nature but all share the same desire for dedication to the Gospel.

Vow of poverty

This is the first of the three evangelical counsels which form the basis of what is traditionally called the religious life. Christians who dedicate their lives totally to God respond to the advice of Jesus contained in the Gospels. To be a true follower a person has to give up earthly possessions in order to have treasure in heaven. Some Christians do this to show complete trust in God. This enables them to live their lives in the service of others as Jesus did. Being poor themselves they are sensitive to the needs of the poor in a way rich people can never be. This is the origin and meaning of Christian poverty. The best known example of a Christian who recognised the value of poverty is Saint Francis of Assisi. He founded a community called the Franciscans who were so poor that they had to beg for food.

> He was setting out on a journey when a man ran up, knelt before him and put this question to him, "Good master, what must I do to inherit eternal life?" Jesus said to him, "... You know the commandments ..." And he said to him, "Master, I have kept all these since my earliest days." Jesus looked steadily at him and was filled with love for him, and he said, "You need to do one thing more. Go and sell what you own and give the money to the poor, and you will have treasure in heaven; then come, follow me." But his face fell at these words and he went away sad, for he was a man of great wealth.

Mark 10:17-22.

Vow of chastity

This is the second evangelical counsel. In order to follow Jesus his disciples had to give up family life. Monks and nuns take a vow of chastity. Like Jesus they give up sexual relations so do not have a husband or wife, and do not have children. This is also called celibacy. The purpose of celibacy is to allow a person to give complete dedication to the Gospel. Christian husbands and wives have duties to love each other and share responsibilities for their children. This limits what they can do to promote the Gospel and to live in service to others. There used to be a belief that the pleasure of sexual and family life distracted a person from the service of God, but since Vatican II Catholics emphasise that marriage is an equal vocation to that of the religious life and celibacy. Mother Teresa is an example of the level of dedication possible to a person who is celibate.

Vow of obedience

This is the third of the three evangelical counsels. Once again it follows the example of Jesus. The New Testament portrays Jesus as being in perfect obedience to God. Christians believe that he died not because he wanted to, but in accordance with God's will. His death is the source of salvation. It would not have been necessary but for human disobedience of God which is sin. Obedience to God includes obedience to human authority because all authority comes from God. Human beings find it difficult to submit to authority because of their pride, but dedicated Christians want to be obedient like Jesus. Christians

RELIGIOUS COMMUNITIES

Two nuns make their profession of vows at Maryfield Convent.

> ... "It is not everyone who can accept what I have said, but only those to whom it is granted."

Matthew 19:12.

They came to a plot of land called Gethsemane, and he said to his disciples, "Stay here while I pray." Then he took Peter and James and John with him. And he began to feel terror and anguish. And going on a little further he threw himself on the ground and prayed that, if it were possible, this hour might pass him by. *"Abba,* Father!" he said, "For you everything is possible. Take this cup away from me. But let it be as you, not I, would have it."

Mark 14:32-36.

who live in a community choose a leader. Just as the original disciples accepted Jesus as their leader so a person is chosen by monks to be abbot or by nuns to be mother superior. The vow of obedience enables a religious community to be united in the service of God and other people.

> Christ proposes the evangelical counsels, in their great variety, to every disciple. The perfection of charity, to which all the faithful are called, entails for those who freely follow the call to consecrated life the obligation of practicing chastity in celibacy for the sake of the Kingdom, poverty and obedience. It is the *profession* of these counsels, within a permanent state of life recognised by the Church, that characterises the life consecrated to God.

Catechism of the Catholic Church (915).

The contemplative life

Contemplation is a state of mind focused on God. The **contemplative** is a person who seeks to live with a permanent awareness of God's presence. It is the vocation of a monk or nun to be contemplative. **Contemplation** requires separation from the everyday world and commitment to prayer. Contemplatives read and meditate on the scriptures in order to understand God's purpose and to experience his love in their lives. They speak to God in prayer, but what God says to them is more important than what they say to God. Saint John of the Cross is a well known contemplative. He wrote about the pain experienced in contemplation. Like Jesus on the cross a person may feel abandoned by God. In modern words this means that a Christian may feel that God does not exist or even worse that God does not care what happens to human beings. Contemplation enables a Christian to experience the whole of life with all its sorrow but also with all its joy.

> Contemplative prayer is the prayer of the child of God, of the forgiven sinner who agrees to welcome the love by which he is loved and who wants to respond to it by loving even more. But he knows that the love he is returning is poured out by the Spirit in his heart, for everything is grace from God. Contemplative prayer is the poor and humble surrender to the loving will of the Father in ever deeper union with his beloved Son.

Catechism of the Catholic Church (2712).

Active life

Many people admire the dedication of monks and nuns. A monastic community is a group of individuals pursuing a spiritual journey, but they try to show God's love and compassion by praying for the needs of the world. Usually even the most traditional religious communities also give some active service. Benedictine monks, for example, provide education in their schools. Mother Teresa has shown how it is possible to combine the contemplative and active life. Her care and compassion for human suffering is motivated by her love of God and her desire to share that love with those desperately in need. All Christians, whether members of a dedicated religious community or not, have to find a balance. They are called to be disciples, that is, spiritual learners who are then sent out as apostles, in love and service to the world.

Examples

There are religious communities of dedicated Christians all over the world. Those founded in the twentieth century often seek to achieve their purpose by returning to traditional practices. The Iona community in Scotland was founded in 1938 by George Macleod as an opportunity for spiritual renewal in awe-inspiring countryside to people who spend their lives in industrial towns. The Taizé community in France was founded in 1940 by Roger Schutz as a new kind of monasticism. The brothers take the traditional vows of poverty, chastity and obedience in order to bring reconciliation to the world. The Corrymeela community in Northern Ireland was founded in 1965 by Catholics and Protestants. Its purpose is to reduce religious prejudice and conflict by bringing Catholics and Protestants together in Christian fellowship. Whatever the particular purpose and practices, all such communities contribute to the establishment of God's kingdom.

Iona Abbey.

St Anthony of Egypt

The Benedictine way of life is one of prayer and it comes from the Christian Gospel. In 270 CE a young man called Anthony went to church and heard the words from Matthew's Gospel 19:21, 'If you wish to be perfect, go and sell your possessions, and give the money to the poor, and you will have treasure in heaven; then come, follow me.' He took the words literally and went out into the desert to live a solitary life of prayer. Other men joined him and they lived together in the desert. They were called monks and their communities were the first monasteries. They needed to be organised and so a written plan of life was devised. Such a written plan of life for monks is called their **rule**. St Anthony of Egypt is known as the father of monasticism.

St Benedict

About 250 years after St Anthony of Egypt, a man living in Italy also felt called to live in the same way. He began as a hermit but soon attracted followers. He established a monastic community for which he wrote a rule. His rule required monks to be poor, chaste and obedient, and to live together in the monastery. His name was Benedict and he began the Benedictine way of life. This was based on the gospel and emphasised Scripture as the basis of the spiritual life for a monk. He required his monastery to be self-supporting and his monks to both work and pray. For St Benedict the purpose of monastic life is to serve God through worship and the community through prayer.

The Benedictines in England

A man in Rome called Gregory was so attracted by the ideals of St Benedict that he founded seven Benedictine monasteries in the city. When he was elected Pope he decided to send a group of 40 monks under the leadership of Augustine to convert the English to Christianity. This Pope is known as St Gregory the

THE BENEDICTINE WAY OF LIFE

Benedictine monks at prayer, Christ the King Monastery, Cockfosters.

Great, and St Augustine became the first archbishop of Canterbury. As well as at Canterbury, Benedictine monasteries were established at Chester, Durham, Ely, Norwich, Peterborough, Westminster, Winchester and Worcester, to name some of the best known. After the dissolution of the monasteries and the foundation of the Church of England, English Benedictine communities continued in exile.

Ampleforth Abbey.

The Abbey of Ampleforth

One of the monks from the original Abbey of Westminster was present when the English Benedictines founded communities abroad. After the French Revolution their property was confiscated and they escaped, this time back to England. St Lawrence's community, which had begun life at Dieulouard, eventually settled at Ampleforth in 1802. It is now an abbey with a large school attached. One of the monks is the headteacher, but most of the teachers are not monks. The school is famous, fee-paying and independent. Its education is modern but still influenced by the Benedictine way of life which comes from the rule of St Benedict. One of the monks of Ampleforth, who used to be a teacher at the school, is the Archbishop of Westminster, Cardinal Basil Hume, OSB.

Work and prayer

The monks of Ampleforth are an example of monastic life in the modern world. Benedict urged his monks to see their call as coming from Christ himself. Like the first disciples they have left everything to follow him. Their response to God is personal but shared through the common life of the monastery under the guidance of the abbot. The monks at Ampleforth live lives of prayer together but they also have to work to support the monastery. They do this by teaching in the school. The monks follow Benedict in seeing their work of teaching as an expression of their life of prayer. In other monasteries the work is different. It may be farming or craftwork, offering retreats and counselling, or being involved in the ministry of parishes. This all follows the Benedictine principle: *Orare est labore; labore est orare.* Benedictine monks show in their lives that to pray is to work and to work is to pray.

Mother Teresa

Mother Teresa was born Agnes Gonxha Bojaaxiu in 1910. She was born and brought up in Yugoslavia, but at the age of 17 she dedicated her life to God and became a novice at the headquarters of the Loreto nuns in Dublin. When she took her vows as a nun in 1928, she took the name Teresa, after her favourite saint. She was sent to Calcutta to teach geography at a convent school. The children's parents had to pay fees, so they were quite rich, but the school was in a poor area and Teresa saw thousands of poor children who had no chance of an education. Before she could go to help the poor, Teresa spent two years with a nursing order receiving medical training. Then, in 1948, she founded a school for slum children in Calcutta.

When she found children dying in filth in the streets with no one even bothering about them, she decided God wanted her to live alongside the poor and share their lives with them. She saw that many people were dying because they were too poor for medical treatment. To help them she pleaded with the Calcutta City Council and was given a disused Hindu Temple to which she took people who were dying. She hoped that in their last few hours on earth, they would realise that they were loved. The temple soon became known locally as 'The House of the Dying', but Teresa called it *Nirmal Hriday* – 'The Place of the Pure Heart'.

Women came to help her and in 1950 she was allowed to form a new order, 'The Missionaries of Charity'. Teresa became the mother superior and so was known as Mother Teresa. The new order kept the school going and more homes for the dying were set up. In 1957, Mother Teresa began to set up leprosy centres after realising that lepers in India were still treated as they had been when Jesus was alive, despite the fact that a comparatively cheap cure was available.

Mother Teresa's example inspired many other people and the order began to grow. In 1973, the BBC showed a documentary about her work and she began to receive money from people who had seen it. This increase in funds and helpers meant that Mother Teresa was able to set up homes for the dying, children's homes and leprosy centres elsewhere in the world. The assistance increased even more when she received the Nobel Peace Prize in 1979.

Mother Teresa's life has been based on the example and teaching of Jesus, especially the parable of the sheep and the goats and the parable of the Good Samaritan. Her motives can be seen in her description of the work and prayer of the Missionaries of Charity.

THE MISSIONARIES OF CHARITY

Work and prayer

We must join our prayer with work. We try to bring this across to our sisters by inviting them to make their work a prayer. How is it possible to change one's work into a prayer? Work cannot substitute for prayer. Nevertheless, we can learn to make work a prayer. How can we do this? By doing our work with Jesus and for Jesus. That is the way to make our work a prayer. It is possible that I may not be able to keep my attention fully on God while I work, but God doesn't demand that I do so. Yet I can fully desire and intend that my work be done with Jesus and for Jesus. This is beautiful and that is what God wants. He wants our will and our desires to be for him, for our family, for our children, for our brethren and for the poor.

From 'A Life For God', compiled by Lavonne Neff.

Mother Teresa blesses a child at the Gift of Love Home during a trip to Singapore.

A typical day

Mother Teresa has described a typical day for the Missionaries of Charity.

Our lives are centred on the Eucharist and prayer. We begin our day with Mass, Holy Communion, and meditation.

After Mass and breakfast, some sisters go to the home for dying destitutes, some to the leper colonies, some to the little schools we have in the slums, some take care of the preparation and distribution of food, some go visit needy families, some go teach catechism, and so on.

They go all over the city. (In Calcutta alone, we have fifty-nine centres. The home for dying destitutes is only one centre.) The sisters travel everywhere with a rosary in hand. That is the way we pray in the streets. We do not go to the people without praying. The rosary has been our strength and our protection.

We always go in twos, and we come back around 12:30. At that time we have our lunch. After lunch, very often we have to do housework.

Then, for half an hour, every sister has to rest, because all the time they are on their feet. After that, we have an examination of conscience, pray the Liturgy of the Hours, and the *Via Crucis*, 'Way of the Cross'.

At 2:00, we have spiritual reading for half an hour, and then a cup of tea.

At 3:00, the professed sisters again go out. (Novices and postulants remain in the house. They have classes in theology and Scripture and other subjects, such as the rules of monastic orders.)

Between 6:15 and 6:30, everybody comes back home.

From 6:30 to 7:30, we have adoration of the Blessed Sacrament. To be able to have this hour of adoration, we have not had to cut back on our work. We can work as many as ten or even twelve hours a day in service to the poor following this schedule.

At 7:30 we have dinner.

After dinner, for about twenty minutes, we have to prepare the work for next morning.

From 8:30 until 9:00, we have recreation. Everybody talks at the top of her lungs, after having worked all day long.

At 9:00, we go to the chapel for night prayers and to prepare the meditations for the next morning.

Once a week ... we have a day of recollection. That day, the first-year novices go out, because they are the ones who don't go out every day. Then all the professed sisters stay in for the day of recollection. That day we also go to confession and spend more time in adoration of the Blessed Sacrament. This is time when we can regain our strength and fill up our emptiness again with Jesus. That's why it is a very beautiful day.

From 'A Life For God', compiled by Lavonne Neff.

QUESTIONS

Factfile 45 Christian Vocation

1 What is a vocation?

2 Give three examples of different ways of
  following a Christian vocation.

3 Explain what is meant by
  (a) discipleship;
  (b) witness.

Factfile 46 Religious Communities

1 What are the three evangelical counsels?

2 What is the difference between the
  contemplative life and the active life?

3 Name two examples of twentieth-century
  religious communities.

**Factfile 47 The Benedictine Way
of Life**

1 How did the monastic way of life begin?

2 Why is St Benedict important?

3 Describe the way of life of a monk at
  Ampleforth.

**Factfile 48 The Missionaries
of Charity**

1 Why did Mother Teresa leave her
  convent?

2 Describe the work of the Missionaries of
  Charity.

3 "To pray is to work, to work is to pray."
  Do you agree? Give reasons for your
  answer, showing you have considered
  another point of view.

13 RELIGION AND THE MEDIA

INTRODUCTION

When television started in Great Britain all channels were expected to have a large input of religious programmes on Sundays, especially between 10.30 a.m. and 12.00 noon and 6.00 and 7.00 p.m. Most of these programmes were either recordings of church services or hymn-singing type programmes and were known as 'the God-slot'. One of the best known ITV programmes was *Stars on Sunday* when famous stars read their favourite religious reading or sang their favourite hymn. Another was *Highway* in which Harry Secombe visited places around the country talking to Christians and singing religious songs. These programmes often had audiences of more than 8 million.

ITV decided to abandon the evening 'God-slot' in 1994 and use the hour from 6.00 to 7.00 p.m. for ordinary programmes. However, BBC1 still has *Songs of Praise* in 'the God-slot'.

Although ITV has abandoned the 'God-slot' religious broadcasting is still strong on British television. There are Christian worship and religious affairs programmes on Sunday mornings. There are special programmes for religious festivals such as *Lent Meditations, Ramadan Prayers, Jewish New Year Reflections, Diwali Thoughts*. There are religious documentaries such as *Everyman* and *Witness*. Religious and moral issues also feature strongly in many soap operas and serious dramas and films.

Much religious broadcasting now reflects the fact that Britain is a multi-faith society. Christianity remains at the centre of religious broadcasting as it is still the religion of over 80% of the population.

These quotations are from the publicity material which Channel 4 sent to the press before the launch of their *Witness* documentary series. Religious broadcasting in some form will continue to be important.

Sir Harry Secombe meets actor Robert Hardy, star of 'All Creatures Great and Small', on 'Highway'.

At a time when religious broadcasting is being increasingly marginalised, particularly with the abolition of ITV's God Slot, Channel 4 is renewing its commitment to religious broadcasting by launching *Witness*, a prestigious new strand of documentaries about personal belief and scheduling them in peak time at 9.00 p.m. There has never been a major strand like this in peak time before – the BBC's Sunday religious documentary strands are much later at night.

Although more British people watch religious TV programmes than attend football matches, there is still a large proportion of viewers who are reluctant to watch programmes of an overtly religious nature. Personal beliefs, however, affect our lives and the decisions we make on an everyday basis ... What previously seemed exclusively religious preoccupations – abortion or euthanasia, for instance – have come to the forefront of contemporary argument.

Religious broadcasting may be in retreat on other channels, but not on Channel 4. *Witness* is our latest initiative and it attempts to do for religion what *Cutting Edge* does for our documentaries.

Michael Grade, former Chief Executive, Channel 4.

Here is a range of religious radio programmes broadcast by the BBC.

BBC RELIGION
Broadcasting at its Best

RADIO 2

Sunday	at 7.00 am	GOOD MORNING SUNDAY
		with Don Maclean
	at 8.30 pm	SUNDAY HALF HOUR
		with Roger Royle
Thursday	at 9.45 pm	THE GOSPEL TRAIN
		with Carol Pemberton
	and PAUSE FOR THOUGHT 7 days a week	

RADIO 3

| Wednesday | at 4.00 pm | CHORAL EVENSONG |

RADIO 4

Sunday	at 6.30 am	MORNING HAS BROKEN
	at 7.40 am	SUNDAY news and current affairs
	at 9.30 am	MORNING SERVICE
	at 11.30 pm	SEEDS OF FAITH
Mon - Friday	at 10.00 am	THE DAILY SERVICE
Thursday	at 9.05 am	THE MORAL MAZE
		with Michael Buerk
Saturday	at 9.50 pm	TEN TO TEN

Also THOUGHT FOR THE DAY and PRAYER FOR THE DAY
Mondays to Saturdays

Plus many other occasional series including THE BIG HOLY ONE with Simon Mayo
on Radio One

WORSHIP AND MAGAZINE PROGRAMMES

BBC 1 had a special 5 minute meditation on Remembrance Sunday 1995 encouraging people to think about the Kohima Epitaph:

'When you go home,
Tell them of us, and say:
For your tomorrow,
We gave our today'

and how past, present and future are intertwined.

Both BBC 1 and ITV broadcast services for special occasions in the religious life of the country.

Meridian TV produced four half-hour programmes leading up to Easter 1993 entitled *Along the Pilgrim's Way*. Debbie Thrower walked along the pilgrim's way from Winchester Cathedral to Canterbury talking to guest pilgrims, such as the Archbishop of Canterbury, about their religious beliefs.

Both BBC and ITV now also produce meditation type programmes (usually fairly late on weeknights rather than on Sundays) whenever there is a religious festival for Islam, Judaism, Hinduism or Sikhism. These programmes tend to focus on members of the faith living in Britain and what the festival means for them.

There is a vast range of religious programmes on television, some appearing every Sunday, others appearing at special times during the year.

Songs of Praise is probably the most famous of the worship-type programmes with a spot on BBC 1 every Sunday between 6.30 and 7.00 p.m.

The programme normally broadcasts from a different locality in the UK each week. A local congregation is arranged in one of the churches and about six popular hymns are sung. A presenter explores the area and interviews members of the congregation about life in the area and how their Christian faith has affected their lives. So the programme contains hymn-singing, some travel features and human interest which you see on programmes like *Oprah*.

A similar sort of mix can be seen in ITV's religious magazine programme *This Sunday* broadcast every Sunday between 10.30 a.m. and 12.00 noon. This usually includes an entire Christian service broadcast live from a church, news from the world of religion and interviews with people in religious news or who have an interest in a current religious or moral issue.

This is a television equivalent of what happens on many local radio stations where a religious affairs programme is followed by a live service.

Such a programme provides a religious service for those who cannot get to church and is a source of interest for churchgoers who may video the programme for its news and interviews section.

BBC 1 also has worship type programmes between 9.00 and 10.00 a.m on Sundays. These can change around the year from *First Light* to *Heart and Soul* to *This is the Day*. They often mix prayers, readings and hymns with interviews about people's religious beliefs.

BBC 1 also has programmes at this time which explore religious issues in a less documentary type way. In *Discovering Eve*, for example, Toyah Willcox explored the feminine side of religion, women's spiritual experiences and whether God should be thought of as female as well as male.

Granada TV has a regular Lenten Meditation series in which prayers, music, paintings, sculptures, readings and interviews are used as guides for meditation on religious themes such as, 'There must be more to life than this', and 'Is death really the end?'.

Documentaries are perhaps the best known of television religious broadcasts because they deal with religious issues as if they were the same as other issues. They also tend to deal with issues which are of major concern to religious people in the UK at the moment.

BBC 1 has a religious documentary every Sunday evening at around 10.30 p.m. – either *Everyman* or *Heart of the Matter*. On Sunday, 26 November 1995, both programmes were broadcast.

Everyman explored the popular but controversial Nine O'clock Service from Sheffield. It investigated how the Church of England allowed a church to develop within a church in an attempt to make services more interesting to young people. The programme used video footage recorded by the Service, and interviews with those involved and leaders of the Church of England.

Heart of the Matter had a panel of experts which discussed the issues raised by the Nine O'clock Service. This programme related charismatic groups within mainstream churches like the Church of England to sects like that involved in the Waco massacre.

Everyman uses a lot of film footage whereas *Heart of the Matter* uses much more discussion to explore an issue. However, they both deal with current religious issues. Programmes in 1995 included the issues of divorce, euthanasia, genetic engineering and the death penalty as well as the more religious programmes.

A VOODOO PRIESTESS IN NEW YORK

22nd Oct 1995

OTHER WORLDS

'Other Worlds' was a different type of religious documentary.

ITV companies often produced a one-off or short series of documentaries with a religious theme. HTV produced *A Dying Order* which observed the daily life of a convent in Warminster, Wiltshire with no apparent future. It simply looked at how the nuns live and noted that where once there were 55 nuns, now there are 16, aged 63 to 104.

The main ITV religious documentary at the moment is Channel 4's *Witness*. It aims to investigate issues which affect 'the individual's search for truth'.

In the first series, *Witness* investigated the poor black churches of South Africa, looking at what types of Christianity could attract so many members. It investigated religion in Los Angeles, from the Church of the Supreme Science whose members see divinity in the atom bomb, to Alcor Life Extension Centre where people who have legally died are deep frozen to be revived at some future date.

In another programme a survivor of the Holocaust faced Neonazi skinheads who deny that the Holocaust ever happened.

BBC 2 has commissioned various religious documentaries which tend to explore particular aspects of religion from a more intellectual angle.

In 1993, for example, BBC 2 produced a series called *Living Islam*. Professor Akbar S Ahmed presented the six programmes filmed in India, Egypt, Nigeria, Turkey, Bosnia, Indonesia, Israel and Great Britain. This series looked at the origins of Islam, its great empires of the past, its struggle with modernity, the role of women in Islam, the difficulties Muslims face in living in non-Muslim societies and what the future holds for humanity.

In the past BBC 2 has been responsible for two great religious documentaries: *The Long Search* presented the world's religions as humanity's search for God, and *The Sea of Faith* looked at how the rise of science and philosophy caused problems for religion.

Channel 4 has produced similar programmes such as *Testament* which looked at the origins and development of the Bible.

FACTFILE 52

RELIGIOUS AND MORAL ISSUES IN SOAPS AND DRAMA

Most people do not think of soaps when they think about religious broadcasting, but because soaps deal with life, they have to deal with religious and moral issues. Many of the issues are of particular concern to Catholics because they deal with areas where the Catholic Church has clear views, e.g. premarital sex, cohabitation, divorce, abortion, euthanasia, homosexuality, celibacy of priests. Soaps also treat specific religious issues like people dealing with death and people becoming religious.

Here are a few such issues from soaps to show you how these programmes can illustrate religious and moral themes.

One of the most famous religious issues was in *Brookside* where Margaret, a young au-pair, sought advice from Derek, a young Roman Catholic priest, and they ended up having an affair.

Neighbours developed a similar theme, but with a very different story line – Annelise wanted a Catholic wedding and made her boyfriend attend classes to become a Catholic. Later, he called off the wedding to become a priest.

Home and Away is full of religious and moral issues; Curtis' problems coping with Lara's death, Angel and leukemia; and Selina and Damien's difficulties with premarital sex and abortion.

An ongoing religious and moral issue on *Coronation Street* has been Ken Barlow's problems as a middle-aged unmarried father. His attempts to marry Denise broke down; she tried to prevent him having access to his son, but he refused to give up, then when they had worked out a way of coping, there were religious problems with the christening.

There have been many dramas on television with very religious themes which you could use for an in-depth study using the same technique as for soaps.

In the early 90s Channel 4 broadcast a major religious drama series. *Brides of Christ* followed two Australian girls in the early 1960s as they became nuns and the religious problems they faced. It was a difficult period – Vatican II changed many practices and reformed the orders and occupations of nuns. A video is available from Channel 4 television.

RELIGIOUS ISSUE – SOMETHING CONNECTED WITH THE MEANING OF LIFE OR WITH A PARTICULAR RELIGIOUS PRACTICE ABOUT WHICH PEOPLE DISAGREE, E.G. HOW TO DEAL WITH SOMEONE DYING, WHO SHOULD BECOME PRIESTS, WHETHER PRIESTS SHOULD MARRY, WHETHER YOU SHOULD ONLY MARRY SOMEONE OF THE SAME RELIGION.

MORAL ISSUE – SOMETHING WHICH IS REGARDED AS THE RIGHT THING TO DO BY SOME PEOPLE AND THE WRONG THING DO BY OTHERS, E.G. DIVORCE, RACISM, ABORTION, EUTHANASIA.

QUESTIONS

Factfile 49 Introduction

1 What was 'the God-slot'?

2 Which programme is still in 'the God-slot'?

3 Give two reasons why Channel 4 decided to put a religious programme on at peak viewing time.

Factfile 50 Worship and Magazine Programmes

1 Watch *Songs of Praise, This Sunday* and one other worship or magazine programme. During and after viewing the programme, answer these questions:
   (a) What is the target audience?
   (b) Why might people in that target audience enjoy it?
   (c) Why might other viewers not enjoy it?

Factfile 51 Religious Documentaries

1 Watch at least two religious documentary-type programmes. During and after viewing write down answers to the following:
   (a) Who might watch a programme like this?
   (b) Why would they find it interesting?
   (c) Did you find it interesting, and why/why not?

2 Have a class discussion on why television produces a wide range of religious programmes.

Factfile 52 Religious and Moral Issues in Soaps and Dramas

1 Watch a soap which is exploring a religious or moral issue. Write down:
   (a) what the issue is;
   (b) why it is an issue for Catholics;
   (c) who is involved;
   (d) how the issue ends.

2 Then answer the following questions:
   (a) Why did the soap deal with this issue?
   (b) In what other ways could the issue have been dealt with?
   (c) How would you have dealt with the issue and why?

RELIGION, WEALTH AND POVERTY

14

Christians believe that wealth is something which can be used for good or evil, and so, in itself, is not a bad thing. Christians should only gain money in lawful and moral ways and when they have wealth, it is a gift from God not theirs alone. Many biblical teachings show that if you have the wrong attitude to money, wealth can lead you away from God:

> True happiness is not found in riches or well-being, in human fame or power, or in any human achievement, but in God alone ....

Catechism of the Catholic Church (1723).

Jesus told a parable about the end of the world when everyone would come before him to be judged. The good and bad would be separated, as sheep and goats are separated by a shepherd. The good would be sent to heaven because as Jesus said, 'For I was hungry and you gave me food, thirsty and you gave me drink ... lacking clothes and you clothed me, sick and you visited me ...' The good people asked when they had ever done this and Jesus said, 'As you did this to one of the least of these brothers of mine, you did it to me.' The bad people were told they were going to hell because they had never fed the hungry, given drink to the thirsty, clothed the naked or visited those who were sick or in prison. When they asked when they had never done these things, Jesus said, 'As you neglected to do this to one of the least of these, you neglected to do it to me.' *(Based on Matthew 25:31-46).*

'For I was hungry and you gave me food ... lacking clothes and you clothed me ...' (Matthew 25:35-36).

FACTFILE 53

CHRISTIAN TEACHINGS ABOUT WEALTH

> People who long to be rich are a prey to trial; they get trapped into all sorts of foolishness and harmful ambitions which plunge people into ruin and destruction. The love of money is the root of all evils ...

1 Timothy 6:9-10.

> Jesus looked steadily at him and was filled with love for him, and he said, "You need to do one thing more. Go and sell what you own and give the money to the poor, and you will have treasure in heaven; then come, follow me." But his face fell at these words and he went away sad, for he was a man of great wealth. Jesus looked round and said to his disciples, "How hard it is for those who have riches to enter the kingdom of God!"

Mark 10:21-23.

> **If anyone is well off in worldly possessions and sees his brother in need but closes his heart to him, how can the love of God be remaining in him? Children, our love must be not just words or mere talk, but something active and genuine.**

1 John 3:17,18.

> **"No one can be the slave of two masters: he will either hate the first and love the second, or be attached to the first and despise the second. You cannot be the slave both of God and of money."**

Matthew 6:24.

In the parable of the Good Samaritan Jesus showed that the commandment to Christians to love God and love their neighbour means they must help anyone who is in trouble whether they live next door or far away (*Luke* 10:25-37).

According to the New Testament our riches should be used for the help of others, especially the poor. Christians believe that all humans are equal in the eyes of God and that all the good things of the earth have been given to us by God to use to help each other. So Christians believe they must share their wealth with the poor:

> God blesses those who come to the aid of the poor and rebukes those who turn away from them ... Love for the poor is incompatible with immoderate love of riches or their selfish use.

Catechism of the Catholic Church (2443, 2445).

This means that the Church is not just concerned about the poor in the UK:

> Rich nations have a grave moral responsibility toward those which are unable to ensure the means of their development by themselves or have been prevented from doing so by tragic historical events.

Catechism of the Catholic Church (2439).

> Particularly since the second world war, countless resolutions and reports have been adopted by the Methodist Conference recognising the obligation laid upon Christians to go to the relief of those in need, to ensure rehabilitation after natural or man-made disasters, and to assist in fundamental development – so as to enable people to become responsible for their own futures.

Methodist statement in 'What the Churches say on Moral Issues'.

FACTFILE 54

THE NEED FOR WORLD DEVELOPMENT

From about 1950 to 1985, it was common to talk of poor countries as 'Third World' countries. This was because some people divided the world into three:
- First World – the West (USA, Western Europe, Canada, Australia, New Zealand, Japan).
- Second World – the communist countries (USSR, Eastern Europe, China). These were regarded as poorer than the West, but richer than the rest of the world.
- Third World – all the other countries, which were regarded as the poorest countries of the world.

Many books may still refer to 'Third World' countries.

More recently, it has become evident that world poverty is a very complex issue. Some countries once regarded as Third World are now richer than the West (e.g. Brunei, Kuwait, Singapore). Others are not as rich as the West, but are not poverty-stricken. So now the countries of the world may again be divided into three groups, but in a very different way:

- developed countries – rich countries like USA and Western Europe;
- developing countries – countries which are becoming richer, like Brazil, Mexico, Malaysia;
- less developed countries (LDC's) – countries which are still very poor and have people starving, like Sudan, Bangladesh, Mali.

Reasons for lack of development

Wars

Many LDC's have been badly affected by wars. In Africa, many civil wars (wars fought between people from the same country) have been caused by European empire-building in the nineteenth century. Consequently, several African races were joined into one country even though half a race was in another country. When these countries achieved independence, they were still artificial countries and one race was often badly treated by the ruling race, resulting in civil war (as happened in Europe when various parts of Yugoslavia were given independence). LDC's can also suffer from wars between countries, e.g. Ethiopia and Somalia, Afghanistan and Russia; and from wars caused by corruption and political differences, e.g. Mozambique, Angola, Guatemala.

Wars destroy crops, homes, schools and hospitals causing even more poverty. They also force many people to leave their homes and become refugees in other safer countries. These neighbouring countries may have been developing, but a sudden influx of refugees with no money or food can make that country poor again.

Natural Disasters

Many LDC's are situated in areas of the world where natural disasters such as earthquakes, floods and droughts are more frequent and more severe than anywhere else. An earthquake or a flood, for example, can destroy many thousands of homes or the farmland on which the inhabitants depend. If rain does not fall, crops will not grow unless you can afford to sink wells, install pumps and organise an irrigation system.

World poverty concerns us all because we are all dependent on each other – if we want the Sudanese to grow cotton for our clothes, we must be prepared to make sure that the Sudanese have enough food.

Debt

Most LDC's have to borrow money from the banks of developed countries to survive and begin to develop. However, these banks charge interest, so that a less developed country can find itself paying more in interest than they earn in foreign currency. In the early seventies, for example, Chile borrowed 3.9 billion dollars. By 1982, she had paid 12.8 billion dollars in interest, but still owed money. This extra 9 billion dollars could have been used to speed up Chile's development. Instead it went to countries that are already rich.

Cash Crops

The only way many LDC's can make enough money for their debts is to grow cash crops (crops grown for sale rather than consumption). Cotton, coffee, tea and tobacco are grown to sell to the developed world. Many people in LDC's are starving because land is used to grow cash crops instead of food.

Other factors contribute to world poverty: lack of education, lack of clean fresh water, disease, low life-expectancy leading to large numbers of children. If a country depends on one major export such as copper or oil and its value falls in the world market, a country may change from rich to poor almost overnight.

Education is an important factor in helping to overcome poverty.

THE WORK OF CATHOLIC ORGANISATIONS TO RELIEVE POVERTY IN THE UK

Every diocese in England and Wales is involved in helping the homeless and those in need, usually through a social care committee. Any information you need can usually be obtained from one of the committees in your diocese.

There is also a Catholic organisation called the St Vincent de Paul Society which helps the poor in the UK. Many parishes have a branch of the Society.

St Vincent de Paul (1580-1660) was captured by pirates in 1605 and enslaved in Tunisia for two years. His experiences there and his readings of the Gospels inspired him to dedicate his life to prisoners and the poor. He founded the Lazarist Fathers (known as the Vincentian Fathers in the UK) and the Sisters of Charity, both dedicated to serving the poor. The fathers are called after the poor man in Jesus' parable, a poor man who is refused help by a rich man. When they die, it is Lazarus who goes to heaven and the rich man who goes to hell.

Parish branches of the Society collect funds and clothes for the poor and visit and help them. In inner city areas they operate soup runs at night, giving warm food to the homeless who are sleeping rough.

CAFOD (Catholic Fund for Overseas Development) was established by the Catholic Churches of England and Wales in 1962 to coordinate the work already being done by organisations such as the National Board of Catholic Women. In 1961, for example, the Board had organised a Family Fast Day. CAFOD is now a major charity with 70 staff at its headquarters and supports 500 development projects in 75 countries.

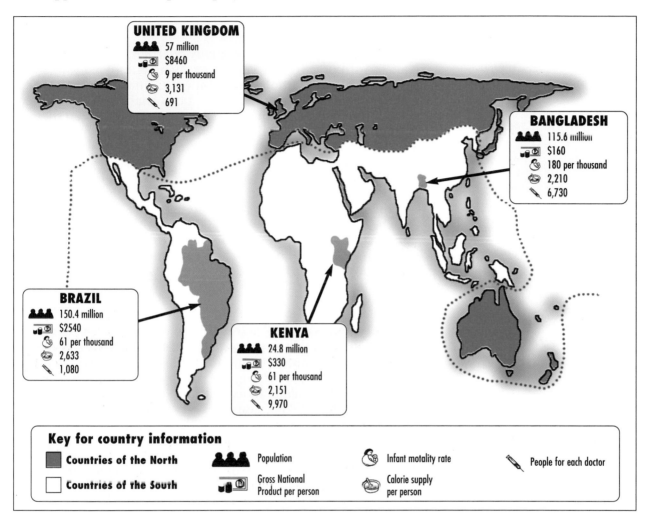

UNITED KINGDOM
- 57 million
- $8460
- 9 per thousand
- 3,131
- 691

BANGLADESH
- 115.6 million
- $160
- 180 per thousand
- 2,210
- 6,730

BRAZIL
- 150.4 million
- $2540
- 61 per thousand
- 2,633
- 1,080

KENYA
- 24.8 million
- $330
- 61 per thousand
- 2,151
- 9,970

Key for country information
- Countries of the North
- Countries of the South
- Population
- Gross National Product per person
- Infant motality rate
- Calorie supply per person
- People for each doctor

CAFOD aims to educate British Catholics about the need for aid, and to raise funds and distribute them to support development projects in the poorest parts of the world. To achieve these aims CAFOD's work can be split into four parts:

1 Fund-raising
In order to do any work to relieve poverty, CAFOD needs money, which is raised in several ways. The main fundraiser is Family Fast Days in Lent and October. There are many other fundraisers, such as: Friday Groups which ask people to give up something and donate the money to CAFOD; 24 hour fasts for young people; and Working in Partnership groups, which raise money for a particular project and get to know the community they are helping. Many churches and individuals also have fund-raising events throughout the year. CAFOD also works with Christian Aid to sell goods produced by LCD's at a fair rate.

Pope John Paul II speaking in Liverpool, 1982.

2 Emergency aid

CAFOD has a disaster fund to deal with natural disasters and refugees which often has to take priority over long-term aid. CAFOD's aid includes: sending food, antibiotics and shelters to flood victims of Bangladesh in the 1995 floods, sending food to drought-stricken Zimbabwe, and sending blankets and food to war refugees in Bosnia and Rwanda. In 1985 CAFOD raised £4.75 million for African famine relief.

3 Long-term aid

CAFOD has an advantage over many charities because it is in contact with organisations at the receiving end of aid through the international Catholic organisation, Caritas. Much of CAFOD's emergency and long-term aid is channelled through Christian organisations in the country concerned. Often these local groups come up with ideas for long-term aid which they ask CAFOD to finance.

The areas around Hola in south eastern Kenya is arid (very dry) and poor. Its 12,000 people make a subsistence living as farmers moving around with their cattle. These people have no access to state health care. Since 1985 CAFOD has been helping the Hola Catholic Mission health programme. During this time three clinics have opened and 40 health workers (chosen by the community and working without pay) have been trained to provide basic medical care and advice on hygiene, nutrition and child health.

In Brazil the richest 10% of its 150 million people receive 53.2% of the wealth, while the poorest 10% of its people receive 0.6%. This has led to about six million homeless children who live on the streets. CAFOD is helping the parish of Piexinhos in Olinda (part of Helder Camara's diocese) to run a scheme known as 'The Community Taking Responsibility for its Children'. Street educators give the children literacy classes and training in skills so that they can earn a living.

In Bangladesh, floods in the district of Khulna often wipe out poor farmers' entire rice crop. CAFOD is helping the Organisation for Peasant Farmers which sets up savings schemes to help them when crops fail and is starting different farmer projects such as duck-rearing units.

4 Education

- About 5% of CAFOD's budget is spent on educating the people and churches of England and Wales about the need for development and the way in which Christians can help less developed countries.
- It publishes a newspaper, *Friday*, and many educational materials. These give information not only about what CAFOD is doing, but also about world development. What the world spends on arms in two weeks, for example, would give everyone in the world enough food, water, education and shelter for a year.

QUESTIONS

Factfile 53 Christian Teachings about Wealth

1 What do Catholics believe is the right attitude to wealth? Give two biblical and two Church reasons for your answer.

2 Which parables did Jesus tell which encourage us to share our wealth?

Factfile 54 The Need for World Development

1 Why do some books refer to poor countries as 'Third World'?

2 Why is it more correct to use the term 'Less Developed Countries'?

3 Make a list of reasons for lack of development.

4 Use an atlas to identify an LDC in Africa, Asia and South/Central America. Check your answers with your teacher.

Factfile 55 The Work of Catholic Organisations to Relieve Poverty in the UK

1 Make a list of the ways in which Catholics help poor people in the UK.

2 Give four reasons why they might do this work.

Factfile 56 The Work of CAFOD

1 Why was CAFOD set up?

2 Make a list of the ways in which CAFOD helps people in Less Developed Countries.

3 Give four reasons why they do this work.

INDEX